STEP UP TO THE PLATE, DAD!

RV BROWN

WINEPRESS **WP** PUBLISHING

Copyright © 2005 by RV Brown.

All rights reserved. No portion of this book may be reproduced, stored in a retrieval system or transmitted in any form or by any means—electronic, mechanical, photocopy, recording, scanning, or otherwise—except for brief quotations in printed reviews or articles, without the prior written permission of the copyright holder, except as provided by USA copyright law.

WinePress Publishing (PO Box 428, Enumclaw, WA 98022) functions only as book publisher. As such, the ultimate design, content, and views expressed or implied in this work are those of the author.

All Scripture quotations, unless otherwise indicated, are taken from the Holy Bible, New King James Version*, Copyright © 1979, 1980, 1982 by Thomas Nelson, Inc., Publishers. Used by permission. All rights reserved.

Scripture references marked NIV are taken from the Holy Bible, New International Version, Copyright © 1973, 1978, 1984 by the International Bible Society. Used by permission of Zondervan Publishing House. The "NIV" and "New International Version" trademarks are registered in the United States Patent and Trademark Office by International Bible Society.

ISBN 1-57921-787-7
Library of Congress Catalog Card Number: 2005901588

Printed in Korea

OVERTON MEMORIAL LIBRARY
HERITAGE CHRISTIAN UNIVERSITY
P.O. Box HCU
Florence, Alabama 35630

DEDICATION

I dedicate this book to my Lord and Savior, Jesus Christ, who has given me the solid-rock foundation on which I stand. This book is also dedicated to my parents, Mary and Willie "Fish" Brown, who gave me the parental training and leadership to become the dad that I am today. Praise His holy name. Amen!

CONTENTS

ACKNOWLEDGMENTS

In writing this book, my hopes and dreams are that men and women who read it will begin to take note of the quality of life and example they are setting before their children. I want to thank Jesus Christ for putting this book on my heart. God started a work in me years ago through my dad. The Lord is continuing that process to this day.

I can't imagine RV Brown writing with such focus on one topic. It is only by the power of the Holy Ghost living inside of me, leading and guiding me every step of the way, that I was able to write this book. Through this experience, I have learned patience and have gained a deeper understanding of God's Word. I have learned how to trust in God's leadership and authority as he gave me the thoughts and meaning behind each chapter. Jesus opened my mind to the most revealing truths in His Word. (I enjoy putting His Word into action and watching the results unfold before my eyes.) Thank you, Jesus!

I want to thank my biggest support group: my wife, Frances; my children, Sommer and Xavier; and my other family members. Frances, my lovely and beautiful wife of twenty-seven years of marriage, endures my travel away from home, manages my office, and most importantly, our family. *Thanks, Sweetpea, for being there for me.* Many thanks to Patricia Robinson-Mitchell, who, along with Frances, revised the book, reading draft after draft, and was faithful to the end. (While I continued sharing the gospel throughout our great nation.)

Many thanks to our friends who helped make this book project a reality. We are eternally grateful.

I am most grateful to Jesus Christ, my Lord and Savior, for allowing me the opportunity to fulfill a life-long dream of writing a book that will impact our society and further the gospel of Jesus Christ, the One who died for me, who rose for me, who said He would comfort me, and come back for me one day. Amen! Hallelujah! Hallelujah! Praise Him!

ENDORSEMENTS

Through God's Word and RV Brown's own personal experience, he gives God's plan for dads to *Step Up to the Plate* to lead their wives, sons, and daughters in the nurture of the Lord Jesus.

In the teaching of God's Word and the work of the Holy Spirit in our lives, we all are being molded into the image of Jesus. This book clearly outlines the stepping-stones that made RV Brown the man of God he is today. You will be blessed and encouraged by reading this book.

—Dr. Danny Lotz and Anne Graham Lotz

One of the great joys of my life is knowing RV Brown . . . RV's commitment, passion, and fervor for the family shows up in almost everything he does . . . I have been in the audience when he has forcefully but compassionately challenged fathers to "step up to the plate" and embrace their God-given responsibility in the home. . . . This burden and mission was nurtured in RV's life from his childhood. . . . And you are holding in your hands the powerful, compelling story of the development and product of RV Brown's calling. . . . As you read through these pages you will be moved, as I am, to be God's man in your home. . . . Thanks, RV, for sharing your heart with us.

—Dr. Crawford W. Loritts, Jr.
Author, Speaker, Host of "Living A Legacy"

RV's story, from the beginning to the present time, has been founded on Scripture. The personal testimony of Carson-Newman College football player Shawn Fletcher testifies to the character of RV Brown.

The challenge is for men to be dads. Give solid, Christlike leadership to your home, your children, and all whom you meet. Truly be a dad or father figure as you live and make a difference in someone's life for Christ.

—Dal Shealy, President/CEO
Fellowship of Christian Athletes

RV Brown is a remarkable combination of qualities, as a man, as a husband, and as a father, that are often separate. RV is simultaneously very strong and very gentle; he is very courageous while admitting that he is very weak without Jesus; he is forthright and direct while still being tactful and sensitive. In a sense, he is like his Master (Jesus Christ). This makes RV an important voice to hear.

—Joseph V. Novenson, Sr. Teaching Pastor
Lookout Mountain Presbyterian Church
and North Shore Fellowship Church
Lookout Mountain, Tennessee

RV Brown's enthusiasm and zeal for God is the "real deal." He will motivate and encourage you to be the kind of father that God wants you to be.

—Pit Gills, M.D. and Director
of (World Triathlon Group) Ironman

1

—ᴓᴓᴓ—

How It All Began

This book is based on the incredible love my father had for me and my sixteen brothers and sisters. My dad was a humble man who loved his family with a godly passion.

Willie "Fish" Brown was my father's name. His family gave him the middle name "Fish" because as a young boy he loved the sport of fishing. He instilled in all of his children the cliché, "Feed a man a fish and he lives for a day. Teach him how to fish and he will live a lifetime." Little did I know that someday I would become a fisher of men. *"And so also were James and John, the sons of Zebedee, who were partners with Simon. And Jesus said to Simon, 'Do not be afraid. From now on you will catch men.' So when they had brought their boats to land, they forsook all and followed Him" (Luke 5:10–11)* Hallelujah!

My daddy retired after working forty years at a fertilizer company in Cayce, South Carolina. When he stopped working, I was six years old. This gave the two of us an opportunity to spend a lot of quality time together. We went fishing, hunting, and talked about the olden days of life. Dad had the ability to speak to me in words that could make things come to life. One time, he was telling me about his favorite fishing hole, how he would get up early to beat the other guys to the fishing spot. Also, he told me about how he dug up worms for bait the day before fishing when other guys would have to dig for theirs on the day of fishing. This lesson was designed to teach me how to prepare myself and not to procrastinate. My father told me his technique was to spit on the worm to make the first fish bite his hook. This idea is still popular. I hear fishermen talk about spitting on the bait and spraying chemicals on their lures to aid in catching fish.

My dad is the champion of the phrase, "Live by example." ***"Train up a child in the way he should go: and when he is old, he will not depart from it" (Proverbs 22:6).*** Dad loved people to the point that our small hometown, Cayce, South Carolina, was a place where everyone knew him and what he stood for. He was always helping someone. He didn't just tell me how to live, he showed me through his communication skills of constantly talking with others, by relating to their life problems, and by setting the example of doing whatever he could to aide them. One example is that of an elderly lady, Mrs. Walker, who lived next door to us. My dad would tell me to help Mrs. Walker with her garden and take care of her yard. Dad had such charisma that he could walk into a crowd of people, and in no time, everyone would be laughing and talking to one another.

My dad would go downtown almost every day to meet his old pals at Phoenix Café. On some occasions, I accompanied him and listened to Dad and his pals discuss their struggles and how God had blessed them to manage these life trials. These conversations had a great impact on my life. I would later tell my wife, when our son was very young, that she should enjoy him now because when he reached the age of five or six, he would be with me.

Willie "Fish" Brown spent time being a role model who taught me how to be a godly man and a dad. *"My son, do not forget my law, but let your heart keep my commands; for length of days and long life and peace they will add to you. Let not mercy and truth forsake you; bind them around your neck, write them on the tablet of your heart" (Proverbs 3:1–3)*. *"When I was my father's son, tender and the only one in the sight of my mother, he also taught me, and said to me: 'Let your heart retain my words; keep my commands, and live. Get wisdom! Get understanding! Do not forget, nor turn away from the words of my mouth. Do not forsake her, and she will preserve you; love her, and she will keep you. Wisdom is the principal thing; therefore get wisdom. And in all your getting, get understanding' " (Proverbs 4:3–7)*. My hope in writing this book is that I can pass on to some other dad the value in not only spending time, but also fellowshipping with his family.

One vital key to my faith and success can be directly related to hearing my parents pray for their children. At night, I would hear my mama praying for all of her children name by name. I would hear my father saying, "Pray for the babies, Mary, pray for the babies." As she would approach my name, I would put my hands over my ears because I wanted to act like the kids down the street. However, Mama would say, "Lord, chastise RV and have him do what you would have him do." Today, so many parents are afraid to pray like my parents prayed. People today say things like, "I would not want my son to be a preacher or some missionary in a strange country." My friend, God's will is going to be done. God has all of the power, and as parents, we need to believe in that power. *"And Jesus came and spoke to them, saying, 'All authority has been given to Me in heaven and on earth' " (Matthew 28:18).*

Growing up in a large family (sixteen brothers and sisters) made my life joyful. Believe me, there was a lot of communication within my family. I feel with all my heart that if families would talk and spend time with one another, the divorce rate in this country would drop dramatically in a short period of time. This can be achieved by putting Jesus at the core of our lives—at the top, on the side, in the back and in the front, to block out Satan. *"So I sought for a man among them who would make a wall, and stand in the gap before Me on behalf of the land, that I should not destroy it; but I found no one" (Ezekiel 22:30).*   **Men, stand up!**

Being next to the youngest in my large family made things a little complicated for me at Lakeview Elementary School, where I attended with most of my older siblings. Teachers would make remarks to me, comparing me to my older siblings, and telling me I needed to be more like one of them. Upon hearing this, I tried to change to be like whomever they compared me to. However, this effort did not work for me. You see, the only person I could successfully be was RV. Sometimes, having a large family worked to my advantage because if someone was bothering me, I could always tell them about all of my brothers and sisters and how they would come to my aid if I needed them.

In the early 1960s, racial integration began, and I jumped at the opportunity to leave my school so that I could be viewed as an individual. Little did I know how dangerous it was being the only minority child in the neighborhood going to a predominately White school. It was tough, and often I would go home severely frightened by the events of the school day. My new school had only four (4) Black students out of approximately 600 to 700 students at R. H. Fulmer Junior High. A lot of times during classes, racial slurs were spoken. One of the most hurtful things for me was to raise my hand, along with other students, when I knew the correct answer, only to be ignored by my teachers. It was hard for me to adjust to this kind of treatment. I began skipping school a lot and not doing my best at all. My seventh-grade school year was very disappointing. I thought by going to a school away from my older siblings that my life would be better. The alternative, however, was that by running from being compared to others, I ran into the ugly face of racism. During this time when I was growing up, I was so disillusioned; I was subjected to name-calling to the point that I did not want to attend school. So, I began to follow kids that did not do their work and ended up failing the seventh grade in school. Also, this was not a situation that my parents knew how to handle.

After failing the seventh grade, I remember that my mother sat me down and told me that I was special. My parents knew I was devastated. You see, that was something my mom and dad did often with me. I don't know about the other siblings, but it made the difference in how I felt about who I was and what I could achieve. My dad said to me that someday I would be a great man at whatever I set out to accomplish. My daddy told me he loved me and would be with me. That was all I needed to hear; this was confirmation for me. That was the beginning of the era of little RV becoming a man. ***"My son, hear the instruction of your father, and do not forsake the law of your mother" (Proverbs 1:8).***

After that time, I became the first African-American to play little league football in Cayce, South Carolina. My brother, Eddie, worked for the Butch Hershey Construction Company, and Butch coached the Little League football team. My brother took me to the Little League practice so I could join the team. I told him that I was not going out on that field to get hurt by those kids. So, my brother said to me, "Here are your choices, either let *them* do it or *I* will do it." You see, Eddie began to live his life through me. The reason I was afraid to play was that I had never seen an actual football helmet in person or anyone wearing a helmet that I could physically touch. That was a big day for me because I did go out on the field after my big brother dressed me in game clothes behind his car in the shopping center parking lot near the playing field. The first few days of playing were rough. I had no idea how to tackle, but I could run, and that was my defense—outrunning the other players. As time progressed, things got better for me. I had purposed in my heart that I was going to be the best running back in the league. That year I made the All Star Team. Being the only Black player at that time made it special for me because my big brother and my family were proud of me.

During the time I was playing with the Little League, there was a special coach by the name of Jones. Coach Jones loved me and gave me rides to and from practice. His attention made me feel special. My second year on the Gold team, Coach Jones had a tragic accident and was burned in a fire. During the years after Coach Jones' accident, I made friends with Faron Spires, Little Joe Smith, David Hildebrand, Sam and Joe Ricker, and Jack Little. These guys will always have a special place in my heart. Especially Faron Spires. Faron's big brother, Donnie, coached us.

You see, if my dad had not instilled character in me, and a passion for life, there would not be an RV Brown today. The time spent with my dad in my early years set a foundation for what I have become. This foundation helped me get through the hard times during middle school. Through all of the turmoil, God had His hand on my life. Success is not easy, but He will make a way. *"I can do all things through Christ who strengthens me" (Philippians 4:13). "And my God shall supply all your need according to His riches in glory by Christ Jesus" (Philippians 4:19).*

My high school years were great. My daddy and mama were proud of me, their son, going to Airport High School in West Columbia, South Carolina. I got involved in everything a student could participate in: FCA, Block-Letter Club, the Student Advancement Club, and other school activities. However, my time was spent developing into an athlete instead of a *student* athlete. My single focus was becoming the best athlete in the school's history. That was a promise I made to myself in junior high school. Well, I accomplished that by lettering in five sports: football, baseball, track, soccer, and wrestling. I don't recall anyone else accomplishing this feat. I was also named Most Valuable Football Player, and Most Superlative Athlete of the Senior Class.

Although I had accomplished so much in sports, I don't remember one person taking the time to talk with me about college athletics, and how I needed to buckle down with my schoolwork. I never visited one college or received one call from a college coach. I made All District Team and numerous news articles were written about my sports ability, without a single phone call or personal interview.

I remember very vividly one day during my senior year of high school, being all of six feet, one-and-a-half inches tall, suffering from *senioritis,* and just overall acting crazy. Coach Richard Smith waited for me until I got out of practice and was walking around the gym. When Coach Smith saw me, he grabbed me in my collar, picked me up, and shoved me against the wall. He said, "Boy, let me tell you something. Being who you are," meaning that I was Black, "You've got a lot to work through, but that attitude you are carrying around here is going to hurt you even more. So you better settle down and act like you have some sense, OK, RV Brown? Do you understand me? Do you understand me?" he asked.

I said, "Yes sir!" You see, Coach Smith was coach for the J.V.'s (the team I played on as a freshman). This was my senior year, and he had continued watching my development. *"My son, pay attention to my wisdom; lend your ear to my understanding, that you may preserve discretion, and your lips may keep knowledge" (Proverbs 5:1–2).*

In my senior year, I received the MVP Award and trophies. However, the Big Fish got away—a scholarship. I was brokenhearted, but God says, "I will always be with you." *"Trust in the LORD, and do good; dwell in the land, and feed on His faithfulness. Delight yourself also in the LORD, and He shall give you the desires of your heart. Commit your way to the LORD, Trust also in Him, and He shall bring it to pass. He shall bring forth your righteousness as the light, and your justice as the noonday" (Psalm 37:3–6).* During that time, my life could have taken a turn for the worst. I could have given up. However, my parents' prayers kicked in, and the glory of God began to work in my life.

After finishing high school, I went to work at the Lance Potato Chip Company. I was eighteen years old and probably the youngest salesman the company ever had. I worked for Lance for a year and then I went to work for Colite Industries Sign Company for a year. Later I worked at South Carolina National Bank Computer Services. At that time we used the IBM 270 and 1320 computers (if my mind serves me right). It was evident that God's hand was on my life. I've made mistakes in my life, but God has never turned His back on me. Even through the down times, He has worked things out in my life. Thank you, Jesus, for loving a wretch like me.

God takes men who give their hearts to Him and turns them into what He calls *His children* and ultimately transforms them into *warriors for His kingdom* (soldiers for Christ). God will lead you and take care of you. *" 'Teaching them to observe all things that I have commanded you; and lo, I am with you always, even to the end of the age.' Amen." (Matthew 28:20).* God worked in my life by allowing me to work at South Carolina National Bank in the computer department. My best friend, Ronnie Hipp, helped me get the job. The computer department was responsible for sorting checks in numerical order. As time moved on, I saw people working in the bank's front office and decided that was where I wanted to work. However, I did not have any formal training to reach that level. Meanwhile, God placed a young man by the name of Timothy Cokely in my life. Timothy told me that I needed to go to college. He told me about a program at South Carolina State College called Planned Education Program. This program later got me focused and on track.

On May 4, 1975, Timothy asked me to take him to Rock Hill, South Carolina, for Winthrop College's graduation. On that day, I met a beautiful young lady named Frances Webster. I still have the piece of cardboard that she wrote her name and phone number on. Little did I know that two years later, Frances would become my wife. It was, indeed, a divine appointment. I thank God for my friend, Pastor Timothy Cokely. The Lord strategically placed this brother in my life. *"A friend loves at all times, and a brother is born for adversity" (Proverbs 17:17)*. Amen.

Portrait of the Brown family. Back row, left to right: Columbus, Willie Ann, Climmel, Kozie, Tony, Helen Shay, Julia, and Terri Ann. Front row, left to right: Eddie, Mama, Daddy, Annie Mildred, and Eloise. RV's mom is holding his picture because he was not present for the photograph. RV was at South Carolina State playing for the National Championship Bicentennial Bowl in 1976. The team was crowned National Champions. Also, missing from the photo are: Ervin, Willie, Theafus, Geneva, and Douglas.

"Behold, children are a heritage from the LORD, the fruit of the womb is a reward."

(Psalm 127:3)

Mama (Mary M. Brown) and Daddy (Willie "Fish" Brown). RV's parents—the ones that started it all! Wow!

Left: Picture of RV during his junior high years—times which he felt were tough. However, nothing stopped him from smiling and pushing on. RV was the first Black student from his neighborhood to attend R. H. Fulmer Junior High (1965).

"No man shall be able to stand before you all the days of your life; as I was with Moses, so I will be with you. I will not leave you nor forsake you."

(Joshua 1:5)

Above: RV's senior high school days (1968–1972) were exciting. He participated in five sports activities: football, wrestling, track, soccer, and baseball. RV lettered in all five sports.

Below: RV also enjoyed playing soccer.

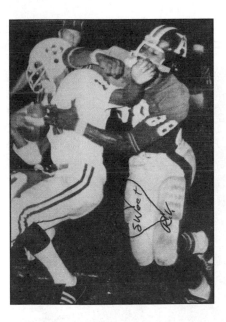

Above: RV enjoyed his football career at Airport High School. He is player number 88.

Left: RV's number two hobby is weight training. He was the first Mr. Physique at South Carolina State College. This is a photo of RV taken during a fundraising project put on by the college's student government to collect food for the needy during the Thanksgiving holidays in 1976.

"Therefore we also, since we are surrounded by so great a cloud of witnesses, let us lay aside every weight, and the sin which so easily ensnares us, and let us run with endurance the race that is set before us, looking unto Jesus, the author and finisher of our faith, who for the joy that was set before Him endured the cross, despising the shame, and has sat down at the right hand of the throne of God."

(Hebrews 12:1–2)

Above: RV continues to maintain his physical strength for battle.

Left to right, RV and brothers: Tony, Kozie, Ervin, Climmel and, Eddie (kneeling). "My family played a major role in my life. Thank God for them." (Photo was taken at a family reunion.)

RV enjoys fellowshipping with his brothers from time to time. Having family ties is the second strongest bond there is, other than a relationship with Jesus—which is number one!

"But if we walk in the light as He is in the light, we have fellowship with one another, and the blood of Jesus Christ His Son cleanses us from all sin."

(1 John 1:7)

Left to right: Ronnie Hipp, Mr. Hipp (Ronnie's Dad), and RV. Ronnie and RV have been friends for more than forty years.

Left: RV fellowships with his friend, Pastor Timothy Cokely. Timothy was with RV when RV met his wife, Frances.

"A man who has friends must himself be friendly, but there is a friend who sticks closer than a brother."

(Proverbs 18:24)

RV met his wife-to-be, Frances Webster, on May 4, 1975. She gave him her phone number and address on this card (shown on the right).

Frances Webster
FoXY
585 5182
128 Hudson St.
Sptbg. 5-4-75

2

THE ROAD TO SALVATION

The first time I sent in my college application, they sent it back to me saying I needed to print my complete name on the form (not realizing that RV Brown is my name). My first name is R and my middle name is V. How about that? After fifteen children, my parents ran out of names. My mama arrived at my name while listening to a soap opera on the radio one day. My mother heard one of the female characters on the show say to her husband, "I love you, RV." When my mama, bless her soul, was about to deliver me into this world, she said, "If I have a little boy, I will name him RV." Guess what happened? Little did she know God would change RV into a mighty man of God. Amen!

When I began college at South Carolina State, I had only enough money for one semester. I knew I could play football, so I began to play in college. At this point in my life, I had not accepted Jesus Christ. However, because prayer was such a part of my parents' lives, I knew what to do to get in touch with Jesus. I prayed and prayed some more. ***"Then He spoke a parable to them, that men always ought to pray and not lose heart" (Luke 18:1).***

Every morning during my first three weeks of college, I would sit on Coach Willie Jeffries' doorstep waiting for him to arrive at work. When he arrived, I would say good morning and introduce myself to him. Each week, he would say, "Come back tomorrow morning." During the fourth week he allowed me to come into his office. He asked the million-dollar question, "Do you have any talent, son, and where did you play football?" He told me to get a physical and report to practice that afternoon. I went across campus yelling out, "Thank you, Jesus! Thank you, Jesus!" My daddy always taught me to give God praise for great things. ***" 'For I know the plans I have for you,' declares the LORD, 'plans to prosper you and not to harm you, plans to give you hope and a future' " (Jeremiah 29:11 NIV).*** So, now you see why God had my daddy and mama pray out loud in the house while I was growing up. Through my dad building character in me early in my life, he planted seeds that had everlasting benefits. ***"But as for me, I will walk in my integrity; redeem me and be merciful to me. My foot stands in an even place; In the congregations I will bless the LORD" (Psalm 26:11–12).*** By waiting for Coach Jeffries and by the coach making me come back over and over again, I learned courage, desire, belief, and most of all, faith. This experience showed me that consistency pays off. ***"Jesus Christ is the same yesterday, today, and forever" (Hebrews 13:8).*** Amen!

Coach Jeffries asked me how I was situated for school. I said, "I have enough for only one semester." He told me how to attain the BEOG (Basic Equal Opportunity Grant) and that the college's athletic department would assist me. I thank Jesus for Coach Jeffries giving me the opportunity to attend college and play football. The next three and one-half years would set the tone for the rest of my life. During my freshman and sophomore years, there was a chaplain named Dr. Nathaniel Griffin who always talked about Jesus and said, "Jesus Christ can help you in the classroom and on the field. He can help you make tackles and help you live right." My thought at that time was, "OK, enough already. I heard that at home. Now I am in college. I don't need this Jesus stuff, because I can take care of myself." How quickly we can forget God's goodness.

I finished my sophomore year in 1977. What a year! Upon returning to college for my junior year, I was a married man—who did not know Jesus. Frances and I were married on June 18, 1977. In November 1977, my wife said we needed to go to church. I said OK, let's go to that chaplain's church and see what he has to say. See, when your parents have been praying for the Heavenly Hound called the Holy Ghost to get on your trail, He won't stop until Jesus becomes the center of your life. So, we went to Dr. Griffin's church, Greater Faith Baptist

Church, where I heard the gospel preached and explained with power and authority. Though I was hard-nosed, I sat up and took notice of the power of God on the chaplain's life and how he was allowing God to use him.

Chaplain Griffin's topic was "What's in hell?" My thoughts were, "Well, I'm a good person. I don't want any part of hell." As the chaplain continued with his message, his movement, his delivery, his voice, and his passion captivated me. I could not move my eyes from him. I listened, focusing on his every word. I hung on to every verse and detail of what I was hearing. Finally, he recited in closing, ***"Where their worm does not die and the fire is not quenched" (Mark 9:44).*** He said, "This means there is no relief, my friend. Now come to Jesus."

At the conclusion of this powerful message, I decided to give my heart and life to Jesus Christ. I gave my wife no warning; I left her still sitting in her seat. I got up and ran down the aisle to the front of the church where a deacon asked me why I had come.

This experience made me think of the following scripture: ***"So He said, 'Come.' And when Peter had come down out of the boat, he walked on the water to go to Jesus" (Matthew 14:29).*** I blurted out, "I don't want to go to hell." The deacon responded by saying, "Well, Son, I will take you into another room so someone can talk to you."

I told him I was not going to take another step without knowing Jesus. As the chaplain walked back and forth, he overheard my conversation with the deacon. Chaplain Griffin came over. He recognized me as a player from the football team. He explained to me what Jesus had done for my sins. On that day in November 1977, I did what it says in the Bible: ***"That if you confess with your mouth the Lord Jesus and believe in your heart that God has raised Him from the dead, you will be saved" (Romans 10:9). "For 'whoever calls on the name of the LORD shall be saved' " (Romans 10:13).*** I accepted Jesus Christ as Lord of my life and Savior of my soul. Hallelujah! Hallelujah! Glory to His name! Amen and amen.

I wish to offer many thanks to Dr. Nathaniel Griffin for leading me to Jesus Christ and for spending two years discipling me. He made me read the book of Proverbs over and over again. He taught me the Word of God. He called it the unadulterated, infallible *Word of God*. He would ask, "Do you understand what I am teaching you?" I grew to have a love and passion for the Word, the Bible, the Truth. I developed a commitment—a desire to grow into what God would have me become. I will be eternally grateful to Daddy Griffin.

Hey, you see, if my dad had not lived righteously before me and prayed with and for me, it would have been hard for me to receive the truth as I did on that day. Dad, *do not,* and I repeat, *do not* take your role in the family for granted. You are vital to your family. *Amen.*

RV enjoys special fellowship with Dr. Nathaniel Griffin, who led him to Jesus Christ at South Carolina State College, Orangeburg, South Carolina.

"My son, pay attention to my wisdom; Lend your ear to my understanding, That you may preserve discretion, And your lips may keep knowledge."

(Proverbs 5:1–2)

The night of baptism, RV prepared himself through the Word of God. "The ray of light in the photo reflects what is truly in my heart, and symbolizes the power of God's Word." Wow!

"Your word is a lamp to my feet and a light to my path."
(Psalm 119:105)

RV (player number 16) and Jessie (player number 15) enjoy a homecoming victory game in 1978. College days at South Carolina State were unbelievable for RV. This time for him was life-changing, future-setting, and a time of development for the leadership that God had in store for him. Hallelujah! All praises go to God!

RV played football all four years while in college and graduated on time (1975–1979). RV Brown is player number 16.

The day RV graduated from South Carolina State College in May 1979. Left to right: Julia, Daddy, RV, Mama, Pearline, Carolyn, Annie Mildred, Tony, and Henrietta.

"The steps of a good man are ordered by the LORD, and He delights in his way."
(Psalm 37:23)

3

—✦—

DISCOVERING GOD'S PLAN
FOR MY LIFE

No more excuses, Dad, for not doing your job of training your family. My dad placed in me the seed of a warrior and taught me that with faith, anything is possible.

I played football all four years of college (from 1975 to 1979), and I graduated after my fourth year. Wow! I did not know what a great thing it was to graduate in four years until I began my teaching career. I learned that most athletes do not graduate in four. I started teaching and coaching in 1979 in the Chattanooga, Tennessee public school system. I continued this career for seven years. In 1983, I was named Coach of the Year for my work with my baseball team. All my desires came true. We were also able to win two district championships and the regional championship in football at Howard High School (a school that I love very much, even to this day).

As a high school athletic coach, I was asked to share my faith often, and I was not afraid to do so. I did this without breaking any rules. It was done for the glory of our Lord and Savior Jesus Christ.

Hey, Dad, it is OK to be successful, but that should not exceed God's plans. My plan was to coach high school for seven years, then reach for the college or professional ranks. Things almost worked out according to my plan. I spent a year as a graduate assistant at the University of Tennessee at Chattanooga (UTC). As a teacher and a coach, I've always believed in stressing the importance of all students achieving their educational goals.

I recall an incident where I was telling the players how to graduate in four years *and* play football. While talking to the players, another assistant coach said to me, "Don't tell them that; we will take care of their education." After this comment, I knew things would have to change for me. I had some tough decisions to make. ***"Seek the LORD while He may be found, call upon Him while He is near" (Isaiah 55:6).*** I got out of coaching for three years and began working with a drug-intervention prevention program called Project 714. The "714" stands for 2 Chronicles 7:14. ***"If My people who are called by My name will humble themselves, and pray and seek My face, and turn from their wicked ways, then I will hear from heaven, and will forgive their sin and heal their land" (2 Chronicles 7:14).*** I loved every minute of my work with this program.

My dad did not know how to read nor did he have any other formal education. However, without having read the passages in the Bible regarding the laws for rearing godly children, my dad was filled by God Himself with the wisdom and common sense of how to love his family and be a good father. I encourage you, Dad, to be strong for your family. Jesus has commanded fathers to understand how important their handprint is on their children's future. Believe me, Dad, God is asking us to be a living sacrifice. Jesus offered us the gift of eternal life by dying on the cross for our sins. If we accept Jesus as our Lord and Saviour, we will be saved. This is the key to having a successful family and building leadership within our communities. *"I beseech you therefore, brethren, by the mercies of God, that you present your bodies a living sacrifice, holy, acceptable to God, which is your reasonable service. And do not be conformed to this world, but be transformed by the renewing of your mind, that you may prove what is that good and acceptable and perfect will of God" (Romans 12:1–2).*

During my seven-year stretch in working in the field of athletics, I had the opportunity to work with an NFL team. The day before I was scheduled to meet with the general manager, he was fired. That action took away my golden opportunity to coach on a professional team. I look at that situation like this; that was a goal I set for myself. However, it was not the will of God for my life. When that happened to me, I knew God was calling me in another direction. *"For the gifts and the calling of God are irrevocable" (Romans 11:29).* I continued to cry out to the Lord for His leading and direction. I knew He had a spiritual plan for my life; I knew He would use me for kingdom building.

For years, I was taught and trained by Pastor Marshall Robinson. I have many sermon dates and notes in my Bible from those precious days of preparation. The Holy Spirit revealed to me the calling of evangelism upon my life in 1985. Pastor Marshall Robinson of Grace Baptist Church, Chattanooga, Tennessee, licensed me as a minister of the gospel of Jesus Christ.

In 1988, I left my teaching and coaching job with the Chattanooga public school system and stepped out on faith into full-time ministry. The Lord gave me the vision to found Outreach to America's Youth, Inc. (O.T.A.Y). In 1991, I was ordained as a minister of the gospel of Jesus Christ by Pastor McKinley Holloway of New United Church of Chattanooga, Tennessee. Several other fine ministers served on my ordination board. Dr. R. C. Reynolds was very instrumental in helping me organize and incorporate Outreach to America's Youth, Inc. Brother Ernie Burgans was always there to encourage and advise me as I embarked on my spiritual journey. I am eternally grateful to each of the fine brothers that poured into my life during those early years of my call to ministry.

God has used O.T.A.Y. to spread the gospel of Jesus Christ throughout the United States of America and other countries throughout the world. *"The Spirit of the Lord GOD is upon*

Me, Because the LORD has anointed Me to preach good tidings to the poor; He has sent Me to heal the brokenhearted, to proclaim liberty to the captives, and the opening of the prison to those who are bound" (Isaiah 61:1).

Dad, the gift of being a father is without a doubt one of God's greatest callings in your life. Don't be afraid to step up and lead. God says in His Word, *"Peace I leave with you, My peace I give to you; not as the world gives do I give to you. Let not your heart be troubled, neither let it be afraid" (John 14:27).* Now, Dad, after hearing those words, you can see there is much power in the Word of the Lord to live by. Allow the Holy Spirit to control your actions. Dad, Jesus is a great provider if you will surrender to His calling. What an opportunity to turn your life over to the hand of God. Do you know how much Jesus desires for that to happen? He desires for you, Dad, to totally surrender your life and your family to Him. Wow!

I want to conclude this portion of the book with a note to my dad. Thank you for the love, gentleness, kindness, and faithfulness you have shown our family. These things have had an affect on me and made me the husband, father, and brother that I am to our family. Words cannot express how much your touch has meant to me.

Thank you, Jesus, for blessing me with an awesome father who loved me and who was a wonderful man that I will always cherish. Thank you, Mama, for all the hugs and kisses I received each morning from you. I thank God for an awesome mother. For these and all other blessings in my life, thank you, Jesus!

Left to right: RV and friend, Minister John Geeter. John was instrumental in assisting with the coordination of programs and events for Outreach to America's Youth for many years.

"And how shall they preach unless they are sent? As it is written: 'How beautiful are the feet of those who preach the gospel of peace, who bring glad tidings of good things!' "

(Romans 10:15)

Left to right: Dr. R.C. Reynolds, RV, and Ernie Burgans. These are men who helped RV launch Outreach to America's Youth in 1987. Dr. Reynolds also challenged RV to step out of his comfort zone and trust God's leading. (RV accepted the challenge. Praise the Lord.) Dr. R.C. Reynolds was RV's Sunday school teacher in 1981.

Above: RV, holding his daughter Sommer, enjoys fellowship with long-time friend Anthony Otey, holding his oldest son, Brian. RV and Anthony worked together at Project 714. Left to Right: Anthony, Brian, RV and Sommer. (Anthony now has a younger son, Adam).

"As iron sharpens iron, so a man sharpens the countenance of his friend."
(Proverbs 27:17)

Bill Sorrells (pictured above with his beautiful daughters) and RV are friends from way back. They coached football together at Howard High School. Left to Right: Johanne, Bill, and Brittaney. (Son, Billy, not pictured)

4

———❧———

DADDY'S INFLUENCE

When my son, Xavier, reached the appropriate age, every chance I had, I carried him along with me. Xavier would not want me to tell you this, but one time when I was preaching at the First Baptist Church of Athens, Tennessee, Xavier stood up during a youth rally. The minute he stood, I knew I was in trouble. He screamed, "Daddy, Daddy, Daddy, I have to go boo boo, Daddy!" Of course, the audience could not contain themselves and broke out into laughter. For me, it is moments like this that I will cherish for a lifetime.

In talking about my children, I cannot leave out my lovely daughter, Sommer. When my children were young, I would sometimes be out of town for a week. After returning, I would take the kids off on a weekend with me so that my wife could have time for herself.

During these times, we would leave home without telling their mom where we were headed, (because oftentimes, I was not sure what we were going to do). I would point and say to the kids, "Nashville is north of us, Birmingham is that way, Atlanta is south of us, and Knoxville, North Carolina, and South Carolina are in that direction." I would let them choose the direction. And, by leaving mom at home, we could skip baths, be messy, and my kids could jump on the beds. My wife believes in picking up and cleaning the hotel room. With no mom around, we could just cut up and have kid-like fun.

Sommer and I also share many special memories. On one of these Dad-and-kids trips, she forgot to take her hair rollers. She said to me, "Dad, what am I going to do?"

Being a creative man, I told her I would take care of the problem. Across the street from where we were staying was a store. I went to the store and got two brown paper bags. I used these bags to cut strips of paper and make rollers like I had seen my sisters do in years gone by.

When Sommer saw what I was doing she said, "Daddy, what are you going to do with that paper?" Of course, she complained when I put the strips of paper in her hair.

However, I told her, "Sommer, in the morning you will have some awesome curls." Also, she cried because I wanted to take a picture of her beautifully rolled hair. I joked with her by saying Buckwheat wore these types of curlers all the time. The next morning when we combed out her hair, she was so proud of the lovely curls.

Dad, nothing helps build confidence in your children more than your embrace. Hug your little girls and tell them how precious they are, Dad. Your holding her signifies your love for her. My wife would always ask me to hold her hand, and I would tease her by saying, "What for? Everyone knows you're my wife." Finally, one day she told me why it was so important to her for me to hold her hand. She said, "My dad never held my hand, and when you hold my hand, I feel the bone in your hand, and it reminds me that I am bone of your bone and flesh of your flesh." *"And Adam said: 'This is now bone of my bones and flesh of my flesh; she shall be called Woman, because she was taken out of Man' " (Genesis 2:23).*

My wife's parents divorced when she was a little girl. My wife went through a lot because her daddy wasn't there. When we got married, I said to her, "You've got to get to know your dad." We began visiting the Webster-Lipford families in North Carolina (my wife's family), and God began to heal the wounds. Praise God! So Dad, you see, you are important in the lives of your children, and do not let society tell you any different. Amen, Dad!

Step up, Dad, and take the leadership role in your precious family. I see so many fathers out in public with their families, and when it comes to saying a blessing, they will make the excuse that they don't like to speak out in public or that the Lord hears their *wife's* prayers. At these times, I watch the wife and children look bewildered that the head of their family cannot ask for blessings on their behalf. The impression I get is that they are saying within themselves, "How sad it is for us that this is our dad."

On one occasion, my son, Xavier, and I were eating at a restaurant, and we prayed together over our meal. When we finished saying our prayer, a son who was sitting with his father at the next table asked his dad why they did not pray over their meal. The father's response was to look at me with anger. However, my job is to set a godly example for my family at all times. I can no longer worry about what man thinks. "Let no man trouble me." *"But Peter and the other apostles answered and said: 'We ought to obey God rather than men' " (Acts 5:29).*

My children know that I get up early in the morning and pray for them. This is a commandment from the Lord; God commands men to step up and pray. *"Rejoice always, pray without ceasing" (I Thessalonians 5:16–17).* My prayer is that any Dad who reads this message will be encouraged to pray without ceasing and to take charge of his family. My intent is to raise a simple question to you: "Do you love your family enough to pray for them and fight for them?" *"And I looked, and arose and said to the nobles, to the leaders, and to the rest of the people, 'Do not be afraid of them. Remember the Lord, great and awesome, and fight for your brethren, your sons, your daughters, your wives, and your houses" (Nehemiah 4:14).* Jesus Christ demands that we take care of our family. He has entrusted them to us.

My dad could not read, but he could write his name. When I learned to read, he would sit me down and say, "Read to me, baby." Then he would call my mama into the room and say,

"Mary, my baby can read," and tears would flow down his face. These times would make me feel proud and affirmed.

The bottom line for us as parents is that we have to respond to the different needs of our children. Dad, you must seek God's understanding and wisdom. In doing so, you will receive spiritual insight, courage, and the ability to reach each child in his own zone. Oh Dad, oh Dad, get into the zone. This means that we need to get into the spiritual side of listening and fellowshipping with each individual mindset of our children's little hearts while they are still tender, young, and willing to absorb the influence and instructions of a dad. *"And you, fathers, do not provoke your children to wrath, but bring them up in the training and admonition of the Lord" (Ephesians 6:4).*

Men, do not waste the early years being so busy that you forget about the little hearts that God has placed in your care. As a man, you are looked to as the protector of your home. You need to spend time in your home and raise your children. Do not hide behind daycare facilities, public/private schools, churches, or the community to do your job as a daddy. You are the father; your role is to teach your family. *"You shall teach them diligently to your children, and shall talk of them when you sit in your house, when you walk by the way, when you lie down, and when you rise up" (Deuteronomy 6:7).* Dad, it is your responsibility to lead and guide your family in the path of righteousness. Take it from a country boy who loved his father and did not want to do anything to hurt that relationship.

Dad, let me share a story with you. Once, after I spoke in a high school in Georgia, a young man from the assembly walked up to me and said, "Will you be my dad for one day?" I have never been so moved in all my life. Man, I tell you what, that touched my heart in a way that made me feel so humble. That young man just wanted to be loved by a man, even if only for one day. Meeting that young man happened some time ago, but I never forgot the words he spoke to me. Man, I cancelled my other appointments and spent the day with that young man.

I feel that the breakdown in American families occurs with fathers who refuse to show leadership and ownership of their family. In today's society, we have a generation of men who lack the necessary skills, wisdom, and confidence to lead their families, because they had no dad to teach and train them. As fathers, we must remember to *pray for wisdom,* understanding, and God's will to be present in our lives. ***"If any of you lacks wisdom, let him ask of God, who gives to all liberally and without reproach, and it will be given to him" (James 1:5).***

Remember Dad, if your dad was not there for you; *be there* for *your* family. Purpose in your precious heart to *forgive* your dad. (Maybe, it was a mother who wasn't there for you. Forgive her, too.)

❖ ***"And be kind to one another, tenderhearted, forgiving one another, even as God in Christ forgave you" (Ephesians 4:32).***

❖ *"But the Comforter, which is the Holy Ghost, whom the Father will send in my name, he shall teach you all things, and bring all things to your remembrance, whatsoever I have said unto you"* (John 14:26 KJV).

❖ *"When my father and my mother forsake me, then the LORD will take care of me"* (Psalm 27:10).

❖ *"Now this is the confidence that we have in Him, that if we ask anything according to His will, He hears us"* (1 John 5:14).

❖ *"Let your conduct be without covetousness; be content with such things as you have. For He Himself has said, 'I will never leave you nor forsake you' "* (Hebrews 13:5).

If you are not communicating with your father or mother, pray for the opportunity to connect with them, if at all possible . . . a chance to get to know them and share Christ with them.

Many dads (and mothers) are heartbroken that they let the years slip by without getting to know their child/children. They would give anything to be reunited with them. My wife, after resuming communication with her father, remembers that he would cry on the telephone and say in a tearful voice, "I love you, baby." She knew her dad loved her. She would tell her daddy that she loved him, too. Though he was not there during her growing up years, God never allowed her to hate her dad. My wife, Frances, has a deep love for her mother and father.

"Children, obey your parents in the Lord, for this is right. 'Honor your father and mother,' which is the first commandment with promise: 'that it may be well with you and you may live long on the earth' " (Ephesians 6:1–3). Though her parents have gone home to be with the Lord, God blessed Frances to develop a strong connection to her dad's side of the family (as well as her mama's side of the family). Though many years were stolen away by the enemy, many life-long relationships with family now exist. One of our most powerful ministers (for our Outreach to America's Youth Retreat) is Pastor Terry Hunt, Frances' cousin on her dad's side of the family. Praise the Lord! God is a restorer. Hallelujah!

RV enjoys reading Bible stories to his babies, Sommer and Xavier.

"Hear, my children, the instruction of a father, and give attention to know understanding."

(Proverbs 4:1)

Frances takes a photo of RV, Sommer, and Xavier having fun with friends at a sleepover party. RV was a mentor for these young men.

Left: RV and family spending time together on a ski vacation in North Carolina.

"And these words which I command you today shall be in your heart. You shall teach them diligently to your children, and shall talk of them when you sit in your house, when you walk by the way, when you lie down, and when you rise up."

(Deuteronomy 6:6–7)

Right: RV and his son, Xavier, having a fun day at the go-cart track in Memphis, Tennessee.

Left: RV and Xavier, hanging out at the beach in Jekyll Island, Georgia.

Below: RV and his daughter, Sommer, enjoy time together at Clearwater Beach in Florida.

Above: RV pulling in his catch—a 350-pound Goliath Grouper fish.

Right: RV's number-one hobby is fishing. Hallelujah! Amen! RV instructs his son, Xavier, on how to reel in a big one!

"My son, hear the instruction of your father, and do not forsake the law of your mother; for they will be a graceful ornament on your head, and chains about your neck."

(Proverbs 1:8–9)

Right: Frances and her father, Carl L. Webster Sr., share a special moment during a family visit to Ferguson, North Carolina. "My dad was very precious to me. I loved him so much."

"And now abide faith, hope, love, these three; but the greatest of these is love."

(1 Corinthians 13:13)

Right: Frances and RV (in the back) with RV's dad and mom (in the front) enjoying fellowship time in Cayce, South Carolina, 1976.

"My son, do not forget my law, but let your heart keep my commands; for length of days and long life and peace they will add to you."

(Proverbs 3:1–2)

The power of influence. Left to right: RV next to his nephew, Xavier (who changed his name to RV), and RV's son, Xavier, and RV's great nephew, Xavier.

"He shall be like a tree planted by the rivers of water, that brings forth its fruit in its season, whose leaf also shall not wither; and whatever he does shall prosper."

(Psalm 1:3)

Left to right: RV and spiritual son, Edwin Lovelady. RV coached Edwin from 1979 to 1980. Twenty-five years later they still have contact with one another. RV performed Edwin's marriage ceremony in 2001.

"Hear, my son, and receive my sayings, and the years of your life will be many. I have taught you in the way of wisdom; I have led you in right paths."

(Proverbs 4:10–11)

5

───❦───

MAMA'S TOUCH

Mothers, I am not leaving you out of this message. You are the tender side of God's grace in the family. Mom, you should remember to always lift up your husband. A lot of men did not receive gratification from their parents. So, wives need to be an encouragement to their husbands. I know for a fact that most successful men today have a good woman backing them up. Mothers need to tell their children that prayer and faith in God are the answers when the family is going through difficult times. There is nothing like a mother's love and influence.

One day as my son, Xavier, was learning to ride, he fell off his bike and came to me crying, "Dad it hurts." I checked his body and found only a little scratch.

I told Xavier, "It's OK. You will be all right." He continued crying and went to his mama (my wife, Frances). She looked at his wound, kissed and rubbed it, and he stopped crying imme-

diately. Children have a positive response to the natural, sooth-
ing touch of their mother.

My wife and I have precious memories of our beloved mothers, Mary Brown and Frances Copeland. Both are home with
the Lord now. My wife, Frances, recalls how her mother strug-
gled as a single mom. "There were six of us. Four of us grew up
in the projects of Phyllis Goins Courts. Times were hard. My
Aunt Estella said, 'Your mama was a *soldier!*' And, I can say, she
truly was a solider. Mama *always* worked. She didn't take any
mess. After completing Spartanburg Methodist College, she became an officer in the South Carolina Department of Correc-
tions. She truly inspired me.

I had many bad experiences in college. Once, my friends
and I attempted to connect with a local church. A man came
up to me after service, handed me a stack of paper slips and
told me to pass them out to all of my friends. The sun was in
my eyes, so I really couldn't see his face. I said, "OK," and he
walked away. When I opened up a slip and read it, it stated,
"This church is for White Only." I was shocked. My friends
and I took the slips to the church pastor, but I couldn't identify
the man.

After several other satanic attacks, I called my mother,
weeping, and begging to come home. I wanted to quit college.
But Mama encouraged me to hang in there and not to give up.
Shortly thereafter, a beautiful card was sent to me by my mother
to encourage my heart. My mother was my sunshine. She gave
our family the motto, 'When doing something great or small,

do it well or not at all.' So, when I take on a task, I do my very best. My mama was my role model. I miss my parents."

❖ *"For His anger is but for a moment, His favor is for life; weeping may endure for a night, but joy comes in the morning" (Psalm 30:5).*

❖ *"And we know that all things work together for good to those who love God, to those who are the called according to His purpose" (Romans 8:28).*

❖ *"And whatever you do, do it heartily, as to the Lord and not to men, knowing that from the Lord you will receive the reward of the inheritance; for you serve the Lord Christ" (Colossians 3:23–24).*

My mother, Mary Brown, was an awesome woman of God who taught us compassion for others. She taught us how to share. One of the most valuable life-skills mama taught us was how to memorize scripture and how to pray.

Mama would prepare meals for us. Many times, there would be ten to twelve of us (or more) at the table. Mama would stand back from the table and begin to pray. At that time I was too young to realize what she was doing. I learned later that she was praying that the food would not run out. It never did.

Mama taught us how to take a stand for what is right and to live godly so that God's blessings would always flow. *"For the LORD God is a sun and shield; the LORD will give grace and glory; no good thing will He withhold from those who walk uprightly" (Psalm 84:11).*

Frances (on the right) enjoys a special evening with her mother, Frances L. Copeland (on the left), celebrating her mother's birthday. "My mother was my heart. I loved her so much."

"She opens her mouth with wisdom, and on her tongue is the law of kindness. She watches over the ways of her household, and does not eat the bread of idleness. Her children rise up and call her blessed; her husband also, and he praises her."
                    (Proverbs 31:26–28)

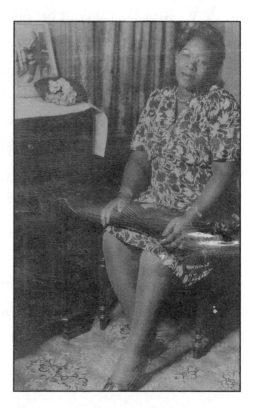

Right: RV's lovely mother, Mary Brown. "My mother was my inspiration and I loved her very much."

6

———

A "Real" Dad

When I look back on my childhood, I can see what a Real Dad should be. A Real Dad is a servant who takes care of his family. A Real Daddy does not have to be a big or robust man, but someone who can truly relate to his family. He laughs and cries with his family. That means he knows the flow of his family and what it takes to get them going in the right direction. A Real Daddy is one who begins his day on his knees praying for his family and the day ahead. He is a husband who prays for his wife's heart and her wellbeing. A Real Dad is one who prays for his children and loves them unconditionally.

A Real Dad puts others first and himself last. *"Let nothing be done through selfish ambition or conceit, but in lowliness of mind let each esteem others better than himself" (Philippians 2:3).* A Real Dad gives of himself to his family, church, and community. I am not talking about giving stuff, but giving of one's self.

Listen up, Dad. A Real Dad reads God's Word (the Holy Bible), believes what he reads, and walks it out. A Real Dad takes God at His word without question. *"Be diligent to present yourself approved to God, a worker who does not need to be ashamed, rightly dividing the word of truth" (2 Timothy 2:15).*

Keep in mind that a Real Dad applies the Word to his life and the way he handles his family. The Word becomes alive in your heart, mind, spirit, and speech. God holds us, Dad, to a different standard. We should be different from other men in the way we walk, talk, and in our beliefs. This difference occurs because we are molded in the image of the Lord and we should not tarnish His Word or the meaning of His holy Word. To do this, we need to live faithfully, insightfully, and be willing to be obedient to the Word of God.

These are God's commandments to us as dads:

1. That we love His Son, Jesus Christ, and keep His commandments. *"For this is the love of God, that we keep His commandments. And His commandments are not burdensome" (1 John 5:3).*
2. That we love our wives with all of our heart, mind, power and appreciate them for what they bring to the table. *"Husbands, love your wives, just as Christ also*

    loved the church and gave Himself for her" (Ephesians 5:25).

3.   That we love our children and teach them how to love and respect God's Word. *"My son, if you receive my words, and treasure my commands within you, so that you incline your ear to wisdom, and apply your heart to understanding; yes, if you cry out for discernment, and lift up your voice for understanding, if you seek her as silver, and search for her as for hidden treasures; then you will understand the fear of the LORD, and find the knowledge of God" (Proverbs 2:1–5).*

4.   That we live the truth before our families and communities. Do this, even though we may make mistakes sometimes. Repent, get up, dust yourself off, and move on to the next level. Never give up, for we have an advocate. *"My little children, these things I write to you, so that you may not sin. And if anyone sins, we have an Advocate with the Father, Jesus Christ the righteous. And He Himself is the propitiation for our sins, and not for ours only but also for the whole world" (1 John 2:1–2).*

Dad, take a stand for what is right! *"And if it seems evil to you to serve the LORD, choose for yourselves this day whom you will serve, whether the gods which your fathers served that were on the other side of the River, or the gods of the*

Amorites, in whose land you dwell. But as for me and my house, we will serve the LORD" (Joshua 24:15).

These are leadership qualities, Dad. *This is called Stepping Up to the Plate!* Your family needs to know where you stand when it comes to Jesus Christ, our Lord and Saviour. Take a stand, Dad; God's Holy Spirit will be with you. God requires a pure heart. *"Blessed are the pure in heart, for they shall see God" (Matthew 5:8).*

Hey, Dad, do you love Jesus today? As you are reading this, begin to allow the Holy Spirit to show you how to change your life and live the way He would have you live. Jesus must be on the throne of your heart. You must receive Him as your Lord and Saviour. Live for Him today. "Tomorrow is not promised to you." *"Do not boast about tomorrow, for you do not know what a day may bring forth" (Proverbs 27:1).*

Hey, Dad, keep it real! You need to fellowship with your family. Spend some quality time with your loved ones.

Some of the ways to fellowship include:

1. Walking in a park – You can enjoy your family's company and the beautiful sight of flowers, trees, water, and fresh air that God has provided for us.
2. Going fishing – God has provided aquatic life, the sounds of water, and environmental beauty for us to enjoy with one another.

3. Participating in sports – Team up with friends or family members in a competitive and wholesome atmosphere, where sportsmanship and godly respect can be learned.

4. Going shopping – economic lessons and values in money management can be developed in order to live a more prosperous life.

5. Attending a movie – You can relax, laugh, and enjoy your family. Life lessons can also be evaluated and discussed in a godly manner.

6. Going for a drive – family members can spend some quality time as they enjoy the beautiful scenery God has provided.

7. Visiting your children's schools – this will strengthen your relationship with your child and keep you grounded in their perspective of life and God's mission for you as a dad.

Dad, being real means getting out of your comfort zone. God is calling us to be a guiding light for our families. This is possible only if we follow *the light* (God's Word). ***"Your word is a lamp to my feet and a light to my path" (Psalm 119:105).*** The Word of God is critical, Dad. *We* should be the lamp-posts in the family, not our wives. So many wives have to take the leadership role in their families; that is out of God's order. Growing up in the country, we had a street lamp in our community, and at night we would gather around the light. Not only would *we* be there under the street light, but also the bugs, mosquitoes, and other night creatures. The light drew our attention. We must light the path for future generations to come by what we say and what we do. Jesus wants to use you as a light in your family, on your job, during your recreational times, in your community, and during your quiet times. ***"You are the light of the world. A city that is set on a hill cannot be hidden. Nor do they light a lamp and put it under a basket, but on a lampstand, and it gives light to all who are in the house. Let your light so shine before men, that they may see your good works and glorify your Father in heaven" (Matthew 5:14–16). "Take firm hold of instruction, do not let go; keep her, for she is your life. Do not enter the path of the wicked, and do not walk in the way of evil" (Proverbs 4:13–14).*** Hallelujah! Hallelujah! Hallelujah!

Hey, Dad, Jesus wants to fulfill His mission in you by blessing your life with a marriage that will be a light in your community. ***"Wives, submit to your own husbands, as is fitting in the Lord. Husbands, love your wives and do not be bitter toward them" (Colossians 3:18–19). "He who finds a wife finds a good thing, and obtains favor from the LORD" (Proverbs 18:22).***

Hey, Dad, Jesus is asking us to rely totally on His Word. Humble yourselves so that Jesus can get the glory out of your life, OK man? *"Therefore humble yourselves under the mighty hand of God, that He may exalt you in due time, casting all your care upon Him, for He cares for you" (1 Peter 5:6–7).* Wow! What a joy to know He cares, my friend. Unfortunately, so many dads have walked away from their families leaving mothers to fend for themselves and their children. If you are a Real Dad, you will not do that because you know that it will not be comfortable for you to watch, from a distance, another man raising your children or your children having to fend for themselves. How sad it is that so many women are put in that kind of situation, which ultimately leads so many young men and women to lives of grief and trouble because they have to carry the burdens of life on their tender shoulders. Dad, I am calling you back home. Even if you are divorced, do whatever it takes to build a relationship with your child or children. Jesus expects that from a Real Dad.

Keep in mind, also, that God is a restorer. He can restore marriages. Our friends, William and Terry Ramsey, are a beautiful example of a divorced couple that God reconciled. The Ramseys remarried on October 22, 1988. What a testimony of God's restoration and healing power. The Ramseys stated that forgiving one another was critical.

Left to right: William and Terry Ramsey.
"Thanks for allowing us to be a part of this blessing. We know without a doubt that this book has been inspired by God. He is truly the author and you are the co-authors. Our prayer is that it will be a blessing to all that read it and it will have a positive impact on many lives."

"Below is one of our favorite scriptures that we have built our relationship on:"

"But seek first His kingdom and His righteousness; and all these things will be added to you."

(Matthew 6:33)

Hey, Dad, we have all made mistakes. Let's own up to it and get it fixed! Jesus and I compel you to do the right thing. Cry out to the Lord; repent of your sins. Go back and mend the little white picket fence that has a broken board in it. Often, this requires talking the situation over and asking for forgiveness. You may need to talk to your pastor or a Christian counselor. Go out and buy the right tools to fix it. Read God's Word, use self-help books, tapes, CDs or whatever it takes to educate yourself in order to "make repairs." *This poor man cried out, and the LORD heard him, and saved him out of all his troubles" (Psalm 34:6). "The LORD is near to those who have a broken heart, and saves such as have a contrite spirit" (Psalm 34:18).* Hey, Dad, getting to work on mending the hearts of your loved ones is one of the most important things you can do before passing on into eternity (death). *"But if you do not forgive, neither will your Father in heaven forgive your trespasses" (Mark 11:26).* I beg you, Dad, get right with your wife, sons, and daughters. Do yourself a favor and don't leave this life without putting the past behind you. *"Brethren, I do not count myself to have apprehended; but one thing I do, forgetting those things which are behind and reaching forward to those things which are ahead, I press toward the goal for the prize of the upward call of God in Christ Jesus" (Philippians 3:13–14).* The highest calling on a dad's life is for him to be filled with the power of the Holy Ghost and for him to be a blessing to his family and others. Nowhere in the Bible does it say it is going to be easy for you as a dad. But, remember that Jesus is your strength.

Dad, it is OK to embrace and kiss your son. Tears fill my eyes as I think of all the young men I visit in prison. They say to me, "If my dad would have just given me a hug every now and then, it would have made a difference in my life. He left my mama and me." Some young men say, "She never told me who my father was." (My eyes are getting heavy now and it is hard to make my fingers move at this moment. My prayer: "Lord, please help me to get through this point in sharing this information with the dads of this world.") I know it must be very difficult growing up and not knowing who your father or mother is. I cannot imagine how that feels. My prayer: "God, please minister to those young men and women that are in the situation of not having a total sense of peace in their lives. Jesus, please fill that void in their hearts with your presence, oh Lord." *"When my father and my mother forsake me, then the LORD will take care of me. Teach me Your way, O LORD, and lead me in a smooth path, because of my enemies" (Psalm 27:10–11).* As my heart is full of sadness for the moment, I know of only one comforter, and His name is Jesus. Thank you, Jesus. Bless your holy name. Amen and amen.

In closing this message, I hope that the information provided helps you to see the need for rekindling the fire within your family. Whether you are married or single, Jesus is standing and waiting for your return to greatness as one of His warriors. I humbly and prayerfully ask you to consider the cost of living without Christ as Redeemer and Saviour of your soul. *"I am the door. If anyone enters by Me, he will be saved, and will go in and out and find pasture" (John 10:9).* Open your heart to the gift that was given on the cross and invite Jesus in. *"If you confess with your mouth the Lord Jesus and believe in your heart that God has raised Him from the dead, you will be saved" (Romans 10:9). "For 'whoever calls on the name of the LORD shall be saved' " (Romans 10:13).* Hallelujah and amen!

National Football League Player, Michael Pittman and his family. Top row, left to right: Melissa, Jordanne, and Michael. Bottom row, left to right: Mykava, Mycah, and Mikey.

RV "Papa" Brown is one of the most inspirational and motivating speakers in the nation. My husband and I met RV and Frances about one and a half years ago at a personal turning point in our lives. We were unbelievably impressed and bewildered why they cared so much about us, without even really knowing us. He helped to guide us in our paths with each other and with Christ. He was the example needed for our family. I grew up not having my father around a lot, and Papa has shown me what the true unconditional love of a father is. I will forever be indebted to Papa and Momma for the strength and love that they have given to my husband and me. They are one of the biggest reasons why our family unit is together and strong today. Papa's passion for Christ and the young men of

America go hand in hand. He creates the urgency and starts that undeniable fire within for Christ in so many young men. He is irreplaceable and is so full of wisdom that you cannot help but hear him. This is his calling and this is his ministry. We love you, Papa! We are so proud to know you and to be a part of your life.

Your spiritual son and daughter,

Michael and Melissa Pittman

National Football League Player, Dexter Jackson and his family. Left to right: Melanise, Dexter, Jazmine, and Daisia Jackson

Mr. and Mrs. Brown have been an inspiration and blessing to our family. They will forever have a big place in our hearts. We love them not only as friends, but also as a mother and father, without whom at times, we feel lost. Whenever we have called upon them either for help or just as motivators to talk to in times of hardship, they have never disappointed us.

RV and Frances Brown shared in all of our special moments. They were there for the birth of both of our beautiful daughters, and have been a very intricate force in their upbringing. On April 26, 2004, there was no question in mind of whom Dexter and I wanted to seal our bond. Without hesitation, RV prolonged his business plans that morning to marry us in the backyard of his home. I remember his words flawlessly. "I felt today was the day. Nothing was going to stop me from marrying you guys this morning." There were moments when I looked over at RV and saw tears in his eyes. He made us truly feel as though he somehow connected with our souls. Through him and his family, the love and blessing of God was certainly amongst us on that special day.

Furthermore, it is without a doubt that Dexter and I have a stronger relationship with God because of RV. He has preached to us the importance of family, fatherhood, and staying connected with our Father in Christ Jesus. Through RV, we have learned patience, the significance of prayer in our home, and what accepting and acknowledging our blessings are all about. We know we have a long journey ahead, but we are determined to keep on the path of becoming closer to God. With RV in our lives, I know we will accomplish that, for he is undoubtedly a true man of God, a great father, and forever a friend.

Melanise and Dexter Jackson and family

National Football League Player, Roman Oben and family. Left to right: André, Linda, Roman, and Roman Jr.

RV Brown has served as a mentor to my family and me for the past two years. He is quite simply the quintessential man of God. Not only does God speak through him, but RV's example as a husband, father, leader, and a man who is one-hundred-percent committed to doing God's work has inspired me to be a better Christian man. RV and his family are truly a blessing from God.

Roman and Linda Oben and sons

National Football League Player Chartric Darby and family.
Left to right: Charlette, Charquise, Charniya, and Chartric.

RV is a strong, godly leader. He is a father, a teacher, a friend, and the people's champ. RV's words of wisdom are powerful, and his light shines everywhere he goes. RV has taught me that the Word of God is my weapon and guide. He taught me to always love my family and to be good to those around me. He always says, "In God there is no failure." RV, I love you, and so does my family. You have truly been there for me and taught me the finer things in life that money could never buy. That is the love of God.

Chartric and Charlette Darby and family

7

─◦◦◦─

SHAWN'S TESTIMONY

Below is a story written by Shawn Fletcher, a young man I met during my journey with the Lord.

The Day that I Met RV Brown

One day in December of 1994, I met an unbelievable man in a gym in Chattanooga, Tennessee. He was huge. He was intimidating. He was awesome. His name was RV Brown. RV heard me from a distance talking to another member of the local gym that we worked out at. All that I talked about was working for an opportunity to play college football. Basically all of that talk was based upon hope and prayers. Little did I know that RV would help me to make that dream come true. I was twenty-two years old, and I had been out of high school for four years. My dream of playing college football looked dim. Yet I just couldn't give up the dream of someday playing college football. RV tapped me on the shoulder with a strange look in his eyes that day. RV mentioned that he had overheard me talking about pursuing college football to another member of the gym. We talked for quite a while as we both worked out that day. RV asked me about my intentions and how I might be able to play college football. RV gave me a lot of hope that day. He assured me that my goals were accomplishable and that he could help. RV seemed to believe in me. I think he could see the passion in my eyes. I just couldn't believe what I was hearing. I was so excited. I still couldn't believe that a man that I had never met would help a total stranger like me. Little did I know that this man had the biggest heart of anyone I had ever met. RV had a passion about him that I had never experienced before. My first impression of RV was, "Awesome," but I thought to myself, "Why in the world would a man who I have never met care so much about helping with my dream?" His passion to help others and his passion for life are unbelievable. I would soon learn that his passion for Christ is that much greater!

It was several months before I would see RV again. Once again, I ran into him at the local gym, and we began to talk. RV made sure that I had his phone number so that I could stay in touch with him.

Jones County Junior College

Within a year, in December 1995, RV was picking me up at five in the morning, and we were on our way to a college called Jones County Junior College in Ellisville, Mississippi, near Laurel, Mississippi. He drove me seven hours to Jones County Junior College (JCJC). On our way to Mississippi we talked about life. We talked about Jesus, and he asked me where I stood with Christ. I learned a lot about RV that day. RV became my stepfather on this day. RV had me enrolled before we left JCJC that day. Once I got into college, I had a choice. A choice to be what God has given me the ability to be. I also had a choice to pack my things up and go home, but as RV said, "If you decide to quit, there is not enough room in Chattanooga for the both of us." He also mentioned the "bat" that he would use on me. I took it upon myself to never let RV down and to take advantage of a once-in-a-lifetime chance that God had given me to pursue my dream.

I attended Jones County for one semester. I loved my college experience there and all that it had to offer, but my heart told me that I was in the wrong place. I had a hard time getting up enough courage to tell RV that I just wasn't interested in continuing college at Jones County. I felt that I had let him down. Once I told RV, he accepted it with a loving smile and said, "I know a place that would be just right for you." I couldn't believe that he didn't hesitate to help me.

Carson Newman College

The college that RV mentioned was Carson Newman. In August 1996, RV drove me to Jefferson City, Tennessee. The drive was much shorter this time (two hours). RV took me up and introduced me to the head coach, Ken Sparks. I was impressed by the school and what it had to offer me—on and off the field. Within a week I was accepted at Carson Newman. I got a chance to get on the football field in the spring of 1997. By the time my career was over at Carson Newman, I had started for three years, played for two national championships, made all South Atlantic Conference as tight end, was chosen to be a member of the football player committee, and I graduated in 2001 with a bachelor's degree in physical education. The knowledge that I gained from Carson Newman is enormous. I learned to be a better man because of the coaching staff at Carson Newman. Ken Sparks based everything around Christ, and because of that, I am a better person today. I gained a few fathers at Carson Newman: Coach Sparks, Turner, Tucker, Deaton, Mitchell, Needs, and many more. Carson Newman was the greatest experience of my life. RV Brown came up to visit the team several times while I was there. Each time, I gained something new. RV was right; Carson Newman was the best thing for me. It was the best experience of my life. My dreams were accomplished at Carson Newman.

Watching RV Make a Difference in Others' Lives

During the college years I would often come home to Chattanooga for the summers. During that time, I got a chance to see RV work with young people. I got to see RV work with my baby brother, Pepper. RV gave me a chance to help him at the Reggie White and Friends camps at the University of Tennessee at Chattanooga (UTC). I also got a chance to visit Fulton High School in Knoxville, Tennessee, with RV as well. RV makes such a huge impact on each person that he comes in contact with. Outreach to America's Youth (O.T.A.Y) is such a great organization. I can't say enough good things about O.T.A.Y. and what RV is doing for America's youth all over the United States. He is a man of God! When RV spoke to the youth, he always gave credit to the pinto beans, cornbread, and collard greens for his enormous arms. I don't know about that, but I know that God made him enormous for the reason he lives today, and that is to preach the gospel and make a difference in everyone's life that he encounters. RV's arms could never compare to the size of his heart or the passion that he has for Christ.

Teacher/Coach

Now I am teaching and coaching in Sequatchie County, Tennessee. I now have an opportunity to make an impact on people's lives the way that RV made on mine. I made a promise to RV to help others the way that he had helped me. I hope that I become a father figure and role model to others the way that RV was for me. I hope someday that someone says that I made a difference. RV made a difference in my life.

My Wedding Day

Just this week, RV drove up from Tampa Bay to take part in my wedding on June 19, 2004. It was such an honor to have RV and Frances. RV was there for me on the most important day of my life. I now live in Ringgold, Georgia, with my wife Amy.

God's Plan

I know now that God had it planned for RV and myself to meet. I have gained one of the greatest friends in the whole wide world. RV is like a father to me. I love this man with all my heart.

Most of all I give thanks to my Lord and Savior, Jesus Christ!

Brandon "Shawn" Fletcher

Man, you see, there are a lot of young people just like my spiritual son, Shawn, was in those early days . . . young people needing truth, direction, and affection. Don't hold back on giving it away. *You Get It, You Got It, and You Give It Away.* This refers to your love, time, and Godly wisdom. (This title was The Fellowship of Christian Athletes' camp theme for the year 2004.) Man, trust me on this; if you come under the control of the Holy Spirit, Jesus can and will use you to build your family. Children need constant affection. Your arms are made to hug, so hug your children over and over again.

Man, Jesus is just waiting to bless your life and supply the insight that is needed for the long haul. Jesus is not a short-term God. He is everlasting to everlasting. *"Jesus Christ is the same yesterday, today, and forever" (Hebrews 13:8).*

To my fellow brethren and men of valor, I will step aside now and allow the words of this message to sink into your spirit, mind, and thoughts. Remember, God loves you, Dad, according to John 3:16. *"For God so loved the world that He gave His only begotten Son, that whoever believes in Him should not perish but have everlasting life."* And, He means it!

Left: Shawn Fletcher and RV at Shawn's wedding. Shawn & RV hold a football to symbolize what brought them together (the game of football, and of course our Lord and Saviour Jesus Christ). RV stood in the gap for Shawn as a surrogate dad.

"And my God shall supply all your need according to His riches in glory by Christ Jesus."

(Philippians 4:19)

Shawn Fletcher at Carson New-man College.

Above, left to right: Amy (Shawn's bride), Shawn Fletcher, RV, and Frances (RV's wife) at the Fletchers' wedding.

"Be anxious for nothing, but in everything by prayer and supplication, with thanksgiving, let your requests be made known to God."

(Philippians 4:6)

8

—⊷⊶⊷—

WHEN A HOUSE BECOMES A HOME

It takes the *power of fathers and mothers working together* to complete our young people's futures. When we do not work as united partners, and we separate our approaches to raising our children, we are more likely to experience failure. In today's society, there is more failure than success in raising children. Part of the cause for this failure is our lack of good communication skills. Parents, I can't stress to you enough the fact that your responsibility to your family is to build your homes upon a solid spiritual foundation. *"Therefore whoever hears these sayings of Mine, and does them, I will liken him to a wise man who built his house on the rock: and the rain descended, the floods came, and the winds blew and beat on that house; and it did not fall, for it was founded on the rock. But everyone who hears these sayings of Mine, and does not do them, will be like a foolish man who built his house on the sand:*

and the rain descended, the floods came, and the winds blew and beat on that house; and it fell. And great was its fall" (Matthew 7:24–27). Parents, you should note that every house is not a home. It takes three things to build a real home: 1) Faith in Almighty God, 2) fellowship time with the family, and 3) truth.

We strive for excellence in our homes by being an example to our families. This is something we build one step at a time. Dad, I beg you not to give in to the excuse that "I don't have time" or "I'm too busy." If *you* don't have the time, I promise you that *Satan will* have the time to destroy you and your family. *"Be sober, be vigilant; because your adversary the devil walks about like a roaring lion, seeking whom he may devour" (1 Peter 5:8).* Dad, Jesus is calling us *to righteousness* and a standard that is not easily penetrated. Also, Dad, take the time to understand the message found in *Colossians 2:6–8: "As you therefore have received Christ Jesus the Lord, so walk in Him, rooted and built up in Him and established in the faith, as you have been taught, abounding in it with thanksgiving. Beware lest anyone cheat you through philosophy and empty deceit, according to the tradition of men, according to the basic principles of the world, and not according to Christ."*

Dad, what I am saying to you is that you must be sold out to your family. I told my wife when we married twenty-seven years ago that I wanted her social security number, so if she ever left me, I could use her social security number to find her. (We always laugh about this.) Before we married, I promised my mother and father and my wife's mother that I would always love and cherish her. That is a promise that I have continued to keep. Of course, there have been some failures in our lives, but none that have caused me to ever want to think about leaving my wife or my home. Though I am intense about my spiritual faith, I enjoy relaxing and having fun with my kids and my wife. (There has to be a balance.) Dad, it takes time to develop into what Jesus would have us become. Therefore, as a father and a man, you should take the time to read the Bible (God's instructions for our lives—the Word.) ***"Study to show thyself approved unto God, a workman that needeth not to be ashamed, rightly dividing the word of truth" (2 Timothy 2:15 KJV).*** The words of life in the Bible will help you grow into the husband and dad that the Lord will be proud of. You will not be subject to the rules of this society in which we live. Always place your trust in the Bible. Dad, allow the Holy Spirit to be your instructor. Stay under the tutelage of the Word of God, and in time, God will reveal His plan for your life. The bottom line is that He (Jesus) loved and cared about you so much that He sacrificed His life for you.

Though my Dad was uneducated, he was a successful father who could relate to his children. I was one of the youngest in my family, but I did not judge my father by his level of education. I loved and learned from a warm-hearted man—my Daddy.

—◦◦◦—

Train Them Up

My father would discipline us in various ways that came without warning. He would tell me something to do, and if I did not respond to his request, he would sneak up on me, and before I knew it, he was laying on the punishment. Then he would explain why he disciplined me in that manner. He would finally say to me, "Life is full of surprises, OK?" However, through his discipline and explanations for punishment, I learned how much he cared for me and my brothers and sisters. " *'For whom the LORD loves He chastens, and scourges every son whom He receives.' If you endure chastening, God deals with you as with sons; for what son is there whom a father does not chasten?" (Hebrews 12:6–7).* Our Dad's discipline showed that he cared enough about us to teach us right from wrong. *"The rod and rebuke give wisdom, but a child left to himself brings shame to his mother" (Proverbs 29:15). "Chasten thy son while there is hope, and let not thy soul spare for his crying" (Proverbs 19:18 KJV).*

Today's young people need good discipline, *not abuse.* When Dad disciplined us, he did it to build character in us for the future. This discipline laid a foundation for good character in following guidelines at home, in school, on the job, and in the community. Dad, when a father loves, respects, and trains his children, he is being obedient to God's command found in *Ephesians 6:4: "And you, fathers, do not provoke your chil-*

dren to wrath, but bring them up in the training and admonition of the Lord." Jesus expects fathers to lead their families. However, many dads in today's society *do not have the backbone to step up to the plate to provide that leadership.* Dad, it is your responsibility to teach your family and *train them up.* **"Train up a child in the way he should go, and when he is old he will not depart from it" (Proverbs 22:6).** Amen and hallelujah! Praise His holy name.

RV and his wife, Frances, during their dating years in Spartanburg, South Carolina in 1976.

"In all your ways acknowledge Him, and He shall direct your paths."
(Proverbs 3:6)

RV and Frances' "first prom" at Brainerd High School in 1980, where RV was a teacher and a coach.

June 18, 1977
Two hearts becoming *ONE* through Jesus Christ and the Word.

"Therefore a man shall leave his father and mother and be joined to his wife, and they shall become one flesh."

(Genesis 2:24)

Our new journey, as *ONE,* begins. My dad's influence, of making his marriage to my mom work, and my relationship with Jesus Christ, gives me the inner strength, confidence, and survival skills needed to be successful in my marriage.

"Can two walk together, unless they are agreed?"

(Amos 3:3)

9

—⚬⚬⚬—

THE GREATEST STEPDAD!

The Blended Family
(Closing the Gap)

Many men today have the responsibility of a blended family. Society often calls these men stepdads, but they are dads when they step up and take care of their family. I want to tell you that Jesus will help you and strengthen you for the task of pulling the two families together. *"But may the God of all grace, who called us to His eternal glory by Christ Jesus, after you have suffered a while, perfect, establish, strengthen, and settle you" (1 Peter 5:10).*

The number-one man that comes into my mind is Joseph. *"Now the birth of Jesus Christ was as follows: After His mother Mary was betrothed to Joseph, before they came together, she was found with child of the Holy Spirit. Then Joseph her*

husband, being a just man, and not wanting to make her a public example, was minded to put her away secretly. But while he thought about these things, behold, an angel of the Lord appeared to him in a dream, saying, 'Joseph, son of David, do not be afraid to take to you Mary your wife, for that which is conceived in her is of the Holy Spirit' " (Matthew 1:18–20). Joseph was a mighty man who accepted God's assignment. God wouldn't have allowed His Son to be in the presence of someone that would not take care of Him. Hey, Stepdad, read the account of how God comes and speaks to Joseph. You know that had to be hard on Joseph for God to tell him to marry Mary, since she was already pregnant with Jesus. However, when the Holy Spirit is telling you to do something, God says to you, "Fear not, for I am with you."

Now Joseph could have said, "Lord why me?" God could see his heart, and God knew his character. God knows, and if you step up, He will guide you. Hey, man, if there is a woman that God has allowed to come across your path and you know in your spirit, not your mind or flesh, that God is telling you to begin a relationship with her, then begin immediately to pray and ask God for His guidance as you start this new journey. When I think of Joseph, he had a choice, and he chose to do God's will. When you allow God's will to override yours, blessings will come to you. God will not give you a task without equipping you to complete it.

Hey man, so many things are happening today to the structure of the family. If God is calling you to step up and be a part of some young person's life as a stepdad, then man, just go on and do it! ***"But be doers of the word, and not hearers only, deceiving yourselves" (James 1:22).*** God is calling some Real Stepdaddies to come on up to the plate and be leaders. Jesus is waiting on you to make the first step, and He will draw closer to you and give you the courage and strength to serve Him and your new family. Amen! Hallelujah!

Hey, man, I want you to consider what the Holy Spirit is saying to you right now. Don't allow Satan to steal your joy. Sometimes things happen in your life. However, you must repent, give your past over to the Lord, move on, and allow Him to order your steps and your future. ***"The steps of a good man are ordered by the LORD, and He delights in his way" (Psalm 37:23).*** Man, I want you to stop beating yourself up. Maybe you made a mistake (divorce); God will not hold that against you for the rest of your life. God will forgive you. Man, I tell you that having the presence of Jesus Christ in your life will make all the difference to those that are around you. David said in ***Psalm 51:1, "Have mercy upon me, O God, according to thy loving kindness: according unto the multitude of thy tender mercies blot out my transgressions." "Create in me a clean heart, O God; and renew a right spirit within me" (Psalm 51:10* KJV).*** Take your new or blended family to a new level of worshipping. Hallelujah, hallelujah, praise God! Go on and thank Him for blessing and restoring you to your rightful position in the family as leader, husband, and dad.

Joseph married Mary and protected her so that other people in the community would not put her down or make her feel like an outcast. Men, God doesn't call us to take the easy way out or go around a situation. He calls us to be bold leaders. When I played football, a head-on-collision was the best hit. That hit caused your helmet to hit another player's chest, lifting that running back or receiver off the ground. The impact of that hit could be felt all over the body. So, Stepdad, take it head on. Have a collision with the Word of God and the Spirit of God so you can feel Him all over you. You have got to read God's Word (the Bible) to understand who you are and the position God has placed you in, my brother. God has uniquely given you another opportunity to solidify your ability to raise a family. Your precious family is depending on you, Dad. Man, put your trust in Jesus and begin to walk with Him in the newness of life. ***"Trust in the LORD with all your heart, and lean not on your own understanding; in all your ways acknowledge Him, and He shall direct your paths" (Proverbs 3:5–6).*** What a privilege it is to know Jesus as Lord and Savior. Man, I can't think of any other place I would rather be than in the presence of a holy and loving God. Dad, you have to ask God for strength and courage. When you do this, God will begin to supply wisdom and understanding. I challenge you, Dad, don't go around saying, "These are my stepchildren." When you say that, it makes the children feel different. Just say, "These are my children." Then the children will begin to feel closer to you, Dad. You have the power to transform their lives into what Christ would want for them.

Dad, you may have built your first family on sinking sand. However, I promise, if you rebuild this one on the Solid Rock (Jesus), God will give you strength to carry the load, Brother. Dad, Jesus is the Rock that will hold your family together and supply all of your needs. As the children of Israel needed food and water, God supplied it. *"All ate the same spiritual food, and all drank the same spiritual drink. For they drank of that spiritual Rock that followed them, and that Rock was Christ" (I Corinthians 10:3–4).* Amen and amen. Hallelujah, hallelujah.

Please, man, step up and please God instead of the flesh and the eye. Fellowship with the Lord on a daily basis and watch what God will do in your life. Trust and believe in the Word of God (the Bible), meditate on the Word, and live by it. The results will be blessing after blessing—total success. *"This Book of the Law shall not depart from your mouth, but you shall meditate in it day and night, that you may observe to do according to all that is written in it. For then you will make your way prosperous, and then you will have good success" (Joshua 1:8).* I plead with you, lay it all on the line and watch the power of the Holy Ghost begin to change you and draw you away from the things that Satan has tried to use to destroy you.

Remember man, Satan is *defeated* already. He is a *loser*. Thank you, Jesus!

You see, Dad, the word "step" *really* means closing the gap so that these young people will begin to feel love, warmth, and tenderness. I'm pleading with you, if God is leading you in the direction of a blended family, pray and move forward. Trust God, and He will be with you. The rewards will be great!

10

———⌘———

No Fear, Dad!!

My heart is burdened and saddened about the lack of backbone in many dads today. So many dads are afraid to discipline, to love, and to share their hearts with their families and with others. My word to you, Dad, is to take charge. *Step up and lead.* ***"For God has not given us a spirit of fear, but of power and of love and of a sound mind" (2 Timothy 1:7).*** The Lord knows that the natural man will have fears. However, the Lord wants us to transfer our fears over into His care. You may be saying to yourself, "Now how do I do that?" You do it by putting your trust totally in Jesus and in His leadership through the Holy Ghost. The Holy Ghost is our comforter. ***"But the Comforter, which is the Holy Ghost, whom the Father will send in my name, he shall teach you all things, and bring all things to your remembrance, whatsoever I have said unto you" (John 14:26 KJV).***

Hey, Dad, you cannot be afraid, OK? Jesus may not answer our prayers the way we want Him to, because our requests and deadlines are not always according to God's will or His timing. Remember, Dad, that the Lord's delay is not His denial. You must be willing to turn over control to Him and let Him direct your conversation, your thoughts, and your visions for your family. ***"Then the LORD answered me and said: 'Write the vision and make it plain on tablets, that he may run who reads it' " (Habakkuk 2:2).***

Write your vision, Dad, and make it plain so that your family will know how to pray, and they will watch for the answers to the prayers. Men of God, you must understand what God has placed inside of you. He has put a warrior spirit in you that gets up and moves on God's command. Jesus has given us dads the heavy responsibility of getting the job done. So why have we allowed Satan and the unbelievers of this society to influence us *not* to take charge when God has told us to *take charge?* Why?

Dad, the responsibility of taking charge of your family lies squarely on your shoulders. It is what I call the pack-mule theory. You see, our shoulders are broader than our women and children's shoulders. Remember the old television series called "Grizzly Adams"? In the show, the old miners would have a donkey with everything the miner owned on its back. The donkey balanced and carried the load. So, Dad, I am telling you that you must carry the load. Don't shuck it off on your wife, as so many men in our society are doing today. I plead with you, Dad, to *step up* without reservation and be the man God has called you to be.

Fathers and mothers need to come together on how things are to be done within the family. ***"Can two walk together, unless they are agreed?" (Amos 3:3).*** Fathers and Mothers, do not, I repeat, do not allow your child to play one of you against the other. It is a sad thing to see this happening in families. Satan uses this kind of ploy often to cause a separation or divorce in marriages. Take charge of your children, Dad. Don't be afraid to discipline them. ***"Chasten thy son while there is hope, and let not thy soul spare for his crying" (Proverbs 19:18 KJV).*** Remember that the Word of God was written by inspired men who were moved by the Holy Spirit. Dad, do the right thing. My Dad disciplined his seventeen children, and we all turned out OK. Do not be afraid to apply the messages of the Bible to your life and your situation. Dad, remember God's promise in ***Romans 8:31: "What then shall we say to these things? If God is for us, who can be against us?"***

Now, Dads, that is some power. **Acts 1:8** tells us what happens next: ***"But you shall receive power when the Holy Spirit has come upon you; and you shall be witnesses to Me in Jerusalem, and in all Judea and Samaria, and to the end of the earth."*** This means that Jesus will be with you on the job, in the house, in the city, in the boardroom, on an airplane, or wherever you are; He will be there with you. Also, that verse is telling us not to be quiet. You should open your mouth and step up to share the good things God has done for you and your family. Dads, you must talk about the blessings of God. What an incredible witness we can be for the Lord.

Hey, Dads, remember what the Word states in *Mark 10:48: "Then many warned him to be quiet; but he cried out all the more, 'Son of David, have mercy on me!'* " They told blind Bartimaeus to shut up, but he *refused* to shut up! And mercy was granted to him. Amen! He was given his sight. Hallelujah! We must have that same boldness as we cry out to God for our families and for others. *"And for me, that utterance may be given to me, that I may open my mouth boldly to make known the mystery of the gospel, for which I am an ambassador in chains; that in it I may speak boldly, as I ought to speak" (Ephesians 6:19–20).*

Listen up, Dads, Jesus is looking for men with the passion to take care of their families. Men, read God's holy Word (the Bible). Stand on God's promises. Trust Him, Dad. The Lord is on the throne, my friend, listening for your prayers. Dad, please open up your mind and your soul to the leadership of Jesus.

So many dads are afraid to loosen up; they are afraid to lose control of the situation. (They never had control, anyway.) Lighten up; Jesus is at the steering wheel of life and death. Dad, don't allow Satan to place fear in your heart as you give in to the leadership of the Holy Spirit. Dad, remember the great reward God promises if we abide in Him and His Word. *"If you abide in Me, and My words abide in you, you will ask what you desire, and it shall be done for you" (John 15:7).* Men, we have to get right with God. We must repent of our sins and live according to God's Word. We must hide His Word in our hearts. *"Your word I have hidden in my heart, that I might not sin against You" (Psalm 119:11).*

Dad, do not allow Satan and the wicked of our society to tell you that you cannot live a righteous life. You can if you believe in the power of the blood that was shed on our behalf on the cross at Calvary. Calvary says it all, Dads. Give your hearts to Jesus. Call upon Him. He is waiting to hear your voice say, "Jesus, I believe you died on the cross for my sins and rose from the dead. Jesus, please forgive me of my sins. Please come into my heart; save my soul. I accept you as my Lord and Saviour." *"Moreover, brethren, I declare to you the gospel which I preached to you, which also you received and in which you stand, by which also you are saved, if you hold fast that word which I preached to you--unless you believed in vain. For I delivered to you first of all that which I also received: that Christ died for our sins according to the Scriptures, and that He was buried, and that He rose again the third day according to the Scriptures" (1 Corinthians 15:1–4).* Believe me, Jesus will hear you and you *will* be saved. Dads, remember that nothing but the blood of Jesus can cleanse your heart, mind, and soul. *"And according to the law almost all things are purified with blood, and without shedding of blood there is no remission" (Hebrews 9:22).* You have to believe that and expect the Holy Ghost to move in—and Satan will move out. Oh, what a relief it is to be free! Amen! Hallelujah! Hallelujah!

❖ *"Do you not know that the saints will judge the world? And if the world will be judged by you, are you unworthy to judge the smallest matters?" (1 Corinthians 6:2).*

❖ *"Jesus said to him, 'I am the way, the truth, and the life. No one comes to the Father except through Me' " (John 14:6).*

Salvation is a gift from God. What do I mean by a gift? Jesus paid for it on the cross, so if He paid for it, and we receive it, then it is a gift. Hey, Dad, are you tired of living just any kind of way at home, then going to church and acting like you are "holier than thou?" We as dads can't afford to live a lie at home, because it will cause your children to not want to serve God. See Dad, the impact of a father on his family has eternal consequences for his family.

You see, Dad, Jesus came to set us free from the burdens Satan and society have placed on our lives. *"Then Jesus said to those Jews who believed Him, 'If you abide in My word, you are My disciples indeed. And you shall know the truth, and the truth shall make you free'. . . . Therefore if the Son makes you free, you shall be free indeed" (John 8:31–32, 36).* Amen. God has commanded you to be a living sacrifice *"I beseech you therefore, brethren, by the mercies of God, that you present your bodies a living sacrifice, holy, acceptable to God, which is your reasonable service" (Romans 12:1).* Present your body as a living sacrifice ...a living sacrifice for your family and your community. Take care of yourself, Dad. Eat properly (you need those vegetables—eat in moderation), exercise regularly, and get the proper amount of rest. If you don't take care of your temple (the body), you won't be around to take care of your family. God wants His men to possess the will, desire, and drive to be obedient and continue in His Word. The responsibility of the family lies squarely on the shoulders of the man (dad). *"But if anyone does not provide for his own, and especially for those of his household, he has denied the faith and is worse than an unbeliever" (1 Timothy 5:8).*

Remember that God does everything in order, and His will stands up in any courtroom, household, community, and even in the coffee room at your job (smile). We must be willing to keep it real to the point of being totally submissive to the lordship and leadership of God through the Holy Spirit. *No fear—be real,* Dad *"Be ye followers of me, even as I also am of Christ" (1 Corinthians 11:1 KJV).* Being a follower of Christ doesn't mean you are a wimp. Being a follower of Christ simply means being humble enough to serve a living God; a God who sacrificed everything so that we could live. Satan comes to steal, kill, and destroy, but Jesus came that we might have abundant life. *"The thief does not come except to steal, and to kill, and to destroy. I have come that they may have life, and that they may have it more abundantly" (John 10:10).*

Jesus left His heavenly home—a place of tranquility, love, and joy—and came to live among sinful men. He died for our sins, was buried, rose from the dead on the third day, and ascended into heaven, but promised to return someday to claim His children. There is no greater love than this! *"Greater love has no one than this, than to lay down one's life for his friends. You are My friends if you do whatever I command you" (John 15:13–14).* Hallelujah! That sends chills all over me, Brother; to know that someone loves you, loves me, and our families that much. Doesn't that make you want to serve Him and dedicate your life to Him?

Hey Dads, it's OK to lose yourself into the hand of a living God who will never leave you nor forsake His Word that lives inside of you. If not now, Dad, then when do you put your trust in someone who loves you and is willing to listen to your fears and see your tears? Someone who's "got your back"? He knows your heartbeat, and Dads, your heartbeat should be that of your family. Souls have eternal security through the blood of Jesus Christ, who made the ultimate sacrifice. *No fear—be real,* Dads. Trust in Jesus. *"The LORD is good, A stronghold in the day of trouble; and He knows those who trust in Him" (Nahum 1:7).* Wouldn't you want to spend a lifetime with someone like that, Dad? Man, what a guy Jesus is! For those that have placed their trust in Jesus, expect the best; live for Jesus and you will be transformed into the man Jesus would have you become. Isn't that what you want for your life and your family? *"In hope of eternal life which God, who cannot lie, promised before time began" (Titus 1:2).* Could you trust in someone who not only says something, but can deliver the goods? No doubt!

Dad, checkout God's request in *Titus 2:1–2: "But as for you, speak the things which are proper for sound doctrine: that the older men be sober, reverent, temperate, sound in faith, in love, in patience."* Note also *1 Corinthians 13:13: "And now abide faith, hope, love, these three; but the greatest of these is love."* It says in *James 1:5, "If any of you lacks wisdom, let him ask of God, who gives to all liberally and without reproach, and it will be given to him."*

Dad, *no fear—be real* so that the young men will have a proper role model. *"Likewise, exhort the young men to be sober-minded, in all things showing yourself to be a pattern of good works; in doctrine showing integrity, reverence, incorruptibility, sound speech that cannot be condemned, that one who is an opponent may be ashamed, having nothing evil to say of you" (Titus 2:6–8).*

Dad, Jesus is expecting interest back on His deposit that was made on the cross at Calvary. Dad, oh Dad, oh Dad, Jesus wants us to put in the time to fellowship with our families.

So many men are afraid to fellowship with the family because they do not know what to say or how to carry on a conversation with the family. How sad that is.

I am tired of hearing men say things like, "Well, my Daddy did not talk, so what is the big deal?" If he did not talk to you, then what should you do? You should t-a-l-k to your family. Well, how do you do that? You do it by opening your mouth and praying to Jesus to fill your mouth with words of encouragement, words that impact, words that give life to those that will listen.

First of all, Dad, your relationship must have *no fear and be real.* This means you must have real fellowship with Jesus. That is the key, Dad. I am asking you to make the ultimate sacrifice; be open to the leadership of the Holy Ghost and allow Him to teach you how to love your wife first, and then your children. God says in ***John 10:27, "My sheep hear My voice, and I know them, and they follow Me."*** Dad, when you do this, Jesus will begin to teach you things only He can. Oh Dad, what a fellowship, what a joy divine, and what peace of mind, to follow the leadership of Jesus Christ. Amen, Dads! *No fear—be real.* ***"There is no fear in love; but perfect love casts out fear, because fear involves torment. But he who fears has not been made perfect in love. We love Him because He first loved us"*** *(1 John 4:18–19). No fear—be real.* John wrote, ***"You are of God, little children, and have overcome them, because He who is in you is greater than he who is in the world"*** *(1 John 4:4).* Can you say amen? Can you say amen? *No fear—be real!*

Left: In 1985, RV's family greets him at the airport as he returns home from a Community Intervention Drug Awareness Training Seminar in Minnesota. Left to right: Mama (Frances), Daddy (RV), Sommer Nicole, and Xavier.

"Yes, if you cry out for discernment, and lift up your voice for understanding, if you seek her as silver, and search for her as for hidden treasures; then you will understand the fear of the LORD, and find the knowledge of God."

(Proverbs 2:3–5)

Right: RV enjoys fun time with his precious children, Sommer Nicole and Xavier.

Left: Mortimer Davenport and his family. Left to right: Martez, Mortimer, JaRaé (standing) and La Tonia.

I first met Coach RV Brown in July of 1979 at Brainerd High School. This was the beginning of a wonderful friendship. I enjoyed being around Mr. and Mrs. Brown a great deal. I could tell by their demeanor and personality that they had a true love for the Lord. As a mentor, he taught me discipline and instilled in me the ability to balance sports and everyday life. When I decided to get married, my fiancé and I asked him to perform the ceremony. He was just as excited as we were, because this would be his first wedding. We prayed and then started our first counseling session. He told us if we put God first, then everything else would fall into place.

In May of 2001, I (Mortimer) went into a diabetic coma and things just did not look good. As soon as my wife called

Coach Brown, he came to Tennessee to be with us. We did not know what the Lord had in store for us, but Coach Brown was there, giving his love, support, and continuously interceding on our behalf in prayer. God has truly blessed our lives by Coach Brown's presence. We love him and Mrs. Brown more than words can express. Day or night they are always a phone call away. May God continue to use and bless them in a special way.

With everlasting love,
Mortimer and LaTonia Davenport

Above: RV enjoys time at his home fellowshipping during a fish fry. (left to right) Roman Oben, RV, Chuck Darby, Dexter Jackson, and RV's nephew, Arthur, standing behind RV. RV flexes his muscles and cuts up with his spiritual sons.

"Then He said to them, 'Follow Me, and I will make you fishers of men.' "
(Matthew 4:19).

Below: Brothers in Christ standing together to meet the challenges of fatherhood, accountability, and leadership in the family. Left to right: Clyde Christensen, RV, and Tony Dungy.

"A friend loves at all times, and a brother is born for adversity."
(Proverbs 17:17)

RV and family, left to right: RV, Paige, Xavier, Sommer, Courtney, and Frances.

"Step up, Dad, and bring them home with the Word of God."

"Being confident of this very thing, that He who has begun a good work in you will complete it until the day of Jesus Christ."

(Philippians 1:6)

11

—◦◦◦—

STEP UP TO THE PLATE AND
BRING THEM HOME, DAD!

Step up to the plate and bring your family home, Dad. The bases are loaded with Mama on first base, children on second base, and Jesus on third base. You may ask, why put Jesus on third base? OK, there are two things to consider before we get started here:

1. If Dad gets walked, Jesus comes in first. If Dad gets a single hit, Jesus still comes in first. If Dad strikes out, Jesus is still the closest to him.

2. Dads have to be willing to step up to the plate and not ask for a substitute for strength (power). There is no excuse for the lack of faith. *"I will love You, O LORD, my strength. The LORD is my rock and my fortress and my deliverer; my God, my strength, in whom I will trust; my shield and the horn of my salvation, my*

stronghold. I will call upon the LORD, who is worthy to be praised; so shall I be saved from my enemies" (Psalm 18:1–3).

Hey Dads, our greatest enemy is ourselves. Many times, we refuse to allow the Holy Ghost to lead in our decision-making process. Our society and the world system have taught us that we can rely on and draw from our knowledge and experiences in life. How far is that from the truth? *"Trust in the LORD with all your heart, and lean not on your own understanding; in all your ways acknowledge Him, and He shall direct your paths" (Proverbs 3:5–6).* So, Dad, when you walk out of the dugout (meaning your home), you must be prepared to take on the day, with God's guidance.

Hitting a Home Run:

1. Pray for strength.
2. Pray for your family.
3. Pray for others.
4. Read God's Word.

"Finally, my brethren, be strong in the Lord and in the power of His might. Put on the whole armor of God, that you may be able to stand against the wiles of the devil. For we do not wrestle against flesh and blood, but against princi-

palities, against powers, against the rulers of the darkness of this age, against spiritual hosts of wickedness in the heavenly places. Therefore take up the whole armor of God, that you may be able to withstand in the evil day, and having done all, to stand. Stand therefore, having girded your waist with truth, having put on the breastplate of righteousness, and having shod your feet with the preparation of the gospel of peace; above all, taking the shield of faith with which you will be able to quench all the fiery darts of the wicked one. And take the helmet of salvation, and the sword of the Spirit, which is the word of God; praying always with all prayer and supplication in the Spirit, being watchful to this end with all perseverance and supplication for all the saints" (Ephesians 6:10–18). Trust me, Dad, Satan is coming after your family. Why? Because the family is the first thing God established. Long before there was a church, God created the first family—Adam and Eve. To God be the glory. So, Dad, trust the Word (the Bible) to keep your family informed on how to live a godly and wholesome life in the name of Jesus. Step up to the batter's box and get ready to face the day with the joy of the Lord in your heart. It is hard for me to see men strike out time and time again by putting the bat on their shoulders and never lifting a hand in raising their children.

Hey, Dad, God is going to hold you totally accountable for the upkeep of your family. Jesus has charged you to accept the role in the family of being the spiritual leader. You may feel that you are not well-versed in the Bible, but keep studying, Dad. Find a solid, Bible-believing church where the Bible is preached with power and authority, and get connected. *"Not forsaking the assembling of ourselves together, as is the manner of some, but exhorting one another, and so much the more as you see the Day approaching" (Hebrews 10:25).* God's Word is clear. Dad, God wants His children to live the Word. *"But be doers of the word, and not hearers only, deceiving yourselves" (James 1:22).*

Dad, Jesus wants you to be the lamppost in your home where the family can come and sit at your feet. Is there a place in your home where the children can feel that Jesus will always show up? How about the dinner table? I taught my children that the dinner table is one place where Mama and Daddy can sit and hear what is going on in their lives. We joke, share, laugh, and cut up. Often, we clear the table, bring out the Bibles, pray, and have Bible study. Man, when I was young, we would have some awesome times at the dinner table. Why? Simple. Because everything happened around the dinner table. It was an awesome time of family fellowship. Hey, Dad, your family needs a special place in the home called God's corner.

Mama, you have no idea how important it is to cook for your family. I know many of you have to work, too. However, you can do it. My mother would clean other people's homes and then come home to prepare a meal for her family of seventeen children. How about *that* for a busy mom? There is no more special time for families than dinnertime. One thing we must stop doing is having our children overly involved in outside activities. Often, we are so busy outside of the home that as families we do not have, or *make time* for prayer, Bible reading, or just simply having fellowship with our family members.

When our children were growing up, they did not spend a lot of time at other folks' homes. We did things together, and by doing so, our children learned how to fellowship and pray with us, their parents. Most of the time, difficulties arise when there is no positive interaction going on within a family. What's wrong with a movie and popcorn at home with Daddy and Mama? Why not implement a Family Game Night? Dad, make fellowship a priority for your family. Come on, give it a try and see if the family does not get closer to one another. That is what Jesus would want. Amen. ***"Only take heed to yourself, and diligently keep yourself, lest you forget the things your eyes have seen, and lest they depart from your heart all the days of your life. And teach them to your children and your grandchildren" (Deuteronomy 4:9).*** Amen.

Hey, Dad, *stepping up* simply means I want to lead and be the instrument Jesus uses to *transform my family*. I want to head into the dugout (my home) with God's game plan. ***" 'For I know the plans I have for you,' declares the LORD, 'plans to prosper you and not to harm you, plans to give you hope and a future' " (Jeremiah 29:11 NIV).*** Dad, the playbook has already been written. Pick it up, read it, and absorb its contents.

Jesus requires that a man be found faithful to his calling. *"For the gifts and the calling of God are irrevocable" (Romans 11:29).* God has gifted each of us with the potential of being great dads. *"And now, O Lord GOD, You are God, and Your words are true, and You have promised this goodness to Your servant" (2 Samuel 7:28).* Dad, just be obedient to the game plan. Read it, study it, and just watch God's blessings flow through you to your family. Don't you want your family to be blessed? Of course you do.

I'm sick and tired of seeing dads acting like Jonah, running away from their calling to be dads. *"But Jonah arose to flee to Tarshish from the presence of the LORD. He went down to Joppa, and found a ship going to Tarshish; so he paid the fare, and went down into it, to go with them to Tarshish from the presence of the LORD" (Jonah 1:3).* How many dads rise up early in the morning and leave their families unprotected; not prayed for, not loved on, not a kiss, not a hug? That's why Satan can destroy so many families. Look how many children live in one city and the father lives in another city. I visit young men in prison and listen to their testimonies. How often I hear these words: "If only my father had just been in the next city or town where I could visit with him. I may not have made as many mistakes as I did." Many young people feel displaced, disrespected, disregarded, and discouraged because their father walked away from their family. (I pause as I'm writing this because tears are trickling down my face.) Dad, do you see how important you are to the family and the authority that you bring to the table? Dad, please change your heart about your kids. You may have children in another part of the country. Yes, but they are still part of your body and your life. Do not turn your back on them. Hey Dad, call them up, rekindle the fire in your heart for them, OK? God's grace is always extended toward forgiveness and forgetfulness. Oh, Daddies, turn around and go back to the cross and ask for forgiveness, and you will find Jesus' arms are open wide for returning sons and daughters. Come on, Dad, have a heart. Reach out and pull your children out of the pit, Dad, as only you and God can do.

Many young girls are looking for the love they never got from their father. Daddies, your daughters need your attention. Believe you me, many are out there making mistakes because they never found Daddy's arms, or Daddy's kisses, for that matter. Money cannot replace the void in the hearts of youth who grow up without their daddies. If their lonely hearts could speak, their hearts' cry would be, "Daddy, I love you. Come home, come home to your family." So many fathers are drawn to the city lights, fast living, fast money; Satan always makes things look better than they really are. Satan (the father of lies) always has a way *into* something and *no way out*. Jesus is the *only way*. Jesus can cleanse our ways, mend the broken hearts that cry out day after day, and restore the precious relationships the enemy set out to destroy. Daddy, your children deserve your everlasting touch. Stay in touch with their feelings and their needs.

Hey, Dad, do you know what I like about old Jonah? After three days in the "Great Fish Inn," Jonah repented, God delivered him from the belly of the great fish, and he began to do the will of God. As a result, the city of Nineveh turned to the Lord. **(Read Jonah 1:17 and chapters two and three).** You see, Dad, if God can use one man to turn a city around, how much more can God use one man to impact one family? If you begin to allow the Holy Ghost to control your life, then I know your family will begin to grow the way God intended for it to grow. You see, the price has already been paid with the blood of Jesus. Step up, Dad, be obedient, and serve a true and living God who gave it all for you and your family. Don't let another moment pass by without examining your heart to see how you feel about God's business and His kingdom. God loves you and your family, my friend. Forget not His benefits. Step up to the plate, Dad!

RV at home plate. Prayer, plus the Word, is a winning combination.

But his delight is in the law of the LORD, and in His law he meditates day and night. He shall be like a tree planted by the rivers of water, that brings forth its fruit in its season, whose leaf also shall not wither; and whatever he does shall prosper."
(Psalm 1:2–3)

Step up to the plate and stand on God's Word, with the power of the Holy Spirit leading.
RV and his family, left to right: Courtney, Sommer, RV, Frances, Xavier, and Paige.

"Oh, taste and see that the LORD is good; blessed is the man who trusts in Him! Oh, fear the LORD, you His saints! There is no want to those who fear Him. The young lions lack and suffer hunger; but those who seek the LORD shall not lack any good thing. Come, you children, listen to me; I will teach you the fear of the LORD."

(Psalm 34:8–11)

12

———⟨❦⟩———

BIBLE STUDY TIME

Hey, man, it is time for daddies to take the leadership role in having Bible study. Man, it does not matter whether you have a seminary degree or not. If you are willing to listen to the Holy Spirit, He will guide you into a wonderful time with your wife and children.

Hey, man, trust me. Jesus will allow you to put it all together. Just pray and trust His Word for the answer and wisdom needed for leadership as a godly man, an awesome husband, and a great dad. Remember, God/Jesus/the Holy Spirit + God's Salvation + God's Word + His will + His blessings = the formula for spiritual success = LIFE.

It's time to study the Bible. This is one way in which I have Bible study with my family. This is a Bible study I had with my wife, Frances. She reads a verse, and then I read one. Please fill in the answers as you go through the Bible study. We open with prayer and thanksgiving to the Lord.

121

❖ Frances: *Colossians 2:6–8: "As you therefore have received Christ Jesus the Lord, so walk in Him, rooted and built up in Him and established in the faith, as you have been taught, abounding in it with thanksgiving. Beware lest anyone cheat you through philosophy and empty deceit, according to the tradition of men, according to the basic principles of the world, and not according to Christ."*

❖ After you receive Jesus Christ, what's next?

_____

_____

❖ What does it mean to be <u>rooted</u>?

_____

_____

❖ How can we guard against being taken captive by the vain philosophy and principles of this world? What can we do?

_____

_____

_____

(Discussion)

❖ RV: *Philippians 2:1–5: "Therefore if there is any consolation in Christ, if any comfort of love, if any fellowship of the Spirit, if any affection and mercy, fulfill my joy by being like-minded, having the same love, being of one accord, of one mind. Let nothing be done through selfish ambition or conceit, but in lowliness of mind let each esteem others better than himself. Let each of you look out not only for his own interests, but also for the interests of others. Let this mind be in you which was also in Christ Jesus."*

❖ How does God want us to treat others?

_____

_____

❖ This world system teaches that some people are better than others. What does God's Word say about that?

_____

_____

_____

❖ Our mind (attitude) should be the same as Jesus Christ. What does this involve?

_____

_____

(Discussion)

❖ Frances: *Ephesians 5:19–21: "Speaking to one another in psalms and hymns and spiritual songs, singing and making melody in your heart to the Lord, giving thanks always for all things to God the Father in the name of our Lord Jesus Christ, submitting to one another in the fear of God."*

❖ What things should we give thanks to God for?

_____

_____

❖ Submitting to one another shows _____ for Christ.

(Discussion)

❖ RV: *Ephesians 5:25–28: "Husbands, love your wives, just as Christ also loved the church and gave Himself for her, that He might sanctify and cleanse her with the washing of water by the word, that He might present her to Himself a glorious church, not having spot or wrinkle or any such thing, but that she should be holy and without blemish. So husbands ought to love their own wives as their own bodies; he who loves his wife loves himself."*

❖ Husbands are commanded to _____ their wives as Christ loved the _____.

❖ He who loves his wife loves _____.

❖ Questions for my wife: Honey, am I a loving husband? Do I take good care of you?

_____

_____

_____

(Discussion)

❖ Frances: *Ephesians 2:18–19: "For through Him we both have access by one Spirit to the Father. Now, therefore, you are no longer strangers and foreigners, but fellow citizens with the saints and members of the household of God."*

❖ We are "fellow citizens with God's people and members of God's household." What does this mean?

_____

_____

_____

(Discussion)

❖ RV: *1 Peter 3:7–9 (KJV): "Likewise, ye husbands, dwell with them according to knowledge, giving honour unto the wife, as unto the weaker vessel, and as being heirs together of the grace of life; that your prayers be not hindered. Finally, be ye all of one mind, having compassion one of another, love as brethren, be pitiful, be courteous: Not rendering evil for evil, or railing for railing: but contrariwise blessing; knowing that ye are thereunto called, that ye should inherit a blessing."*

❖ Husbands are commanded to _____ their wives. If they don't, their _____ will not be answered.

❖ What does God say about couples rendering evil for evil; railing for railing (arguing)?

_____

_____

_____

❖ If we bless our mate, we will inherit a _____.

(Discussion)

❖ Frances: *Colossians 3:23–25: "And whatever you do, do it heartily, as to the Lord and not to men, knowing that from the Lord you will receive the reward of the inheritance; for you serve the Lord Christ. But he who does wrong will be repaid for what he has done, and there is no partiality."*

❖ We should do our work as to _____, not to _____.

❖ We are promised an _____ from the Lord as a reward.

❖ Anyone who does wrong will pay the price for his wrong. What do you think about this?

_____

_____

_____

(Discussion)

❖ RV: *Ephesians 4:29–32: "Let no corrupt word proceed out of your mouth, but what is good for necessary edification, that it may impart grace to the hearers. And do not grieve the Holy Spirit of God, by whom you were sealed for the day of redemption. Let all bitterness, wrath, anger, clamor, and evil speaking be put away from you, with all malice. And be kind to one another, tenderhearted, forgiving one another, even as God in Christ forgave you."*

❖ List and discuss all of the behavior God commands us to get rid of:

_____

_____

_____

_____

❖ It is wonderful to know that we are sealed by the Holy Spirit of God for the day of redemption. Hallelujah! Why should I forgive others?

_____

_____

_____

(Discussion)

❖ Frances: *Colossians 3:9–10: "Do not lie to one another, since you have put off the old man with his deeds, and have put on the new man who is renewed in knowledge according to the image of Him who created him."*

❖ God does not want us to _____ to one another.

❖ *"Therefore if any man be in Christ, he is a new creature: old things are passed away; behold, all things are become new" (2 Corinthians 5:17 KJV).*

_____

_____

(Discussion)

❖ RV: *1 Thessalonians 5:16–18: "Rejoice always, pray without ceasing, in everything give thanks; for this is the will of God in Christ Jesus for you."*
(Amen, Brother, amen, Brother—just do it!)

❖ How should we pray?

_____

_____

_____

❖ Should we rejoice and give thanks even during the hard times?

_____

_____

_____

(Discussion)

Questions for my wife:

❖ What can I do to make things smoother around the house?

_____

_____

❖ Do I bring joy to your life?

_____

_____

❖ (Share with my wife how thankful I am for her)

❖ Close Bible study in prayer. (My wife prays, and then I pray.)

Bible Study Time

RV (right) and his son, Xavier (left), having Bible study at home.

"My son, do not despise the chastening of the LORD, nor detest His correction; for whom the LORD loves He corrects, just as a father the son in whom he delights."
(Proverbs 3:11–12)

RV enjoys sharing God's Word with his family. Left to right: Courtney, Frances, Xavier, Sommer, RV, and Paige.

RV, a teacher and lover of the Word of God. RV teaches men how and why they should lead the family and allow the authority of the Holy Ghost to guide and direct their lives. He teaches them leadership skills needed to hold the family together. RV teaches that men should want God's favor.

"For the LORD God is a sun and shield; the LORD will give grace and glory; no good thing will He withhold from those who walk uprightly. O LORD of hosts, blessed is the man who trusts in You!"

(Psalm 84:11–12)

RV and Outreach to America's Youth Today

Recently, Evangelist RV Brown had the incredible, awesome opportunity to go with a group of brothers to the home of Evangelist Dr. Billy Graham. What an honor to spend time with such a mighty man of God!

Evangelist Brown continues to travel throughout the world preaching the gospel of Jesus Christ. In addition to their two children, Xavier and Sommer (now young adults), RV and his wife, Frances, are currently raising two teenage nieces, Paige and Courtney. Though he is very busy, RV makes it a point to spend quality time with his family.

RV and his family attend Grace Family Church (GFC) in Lutz, Florida. The senior pastor is Craig Altman. RV speaks to the *180 Youth Group Ministry* and to the church congregation of GFC periodically.

Outreach to America's Youth, Inc. (O.T.A.Y) sponsors a teen retreat and a marriage retreat annually. Lurone Jennings II is the Director of O.T.A.Y.'s *Breaking the Chain* program. He works with small groups within high school settings. This program is designed to challenge young people to evaluate themselves in terms of where they are and where they would like to go, to assist them in setting short-term and long-term goals, and to promote self-esteem and a positive attitude and outlook for the future. Evangelist Brown continues to conduct chapel services for college and NFL teams. RV also conducts motivational school assemblies throughout the country.

Evangelist RV Brown is humbled that God continues to use him and the Outreach to America's Youth Ministry for kingdom building. He thanks God for the many souls that have been saved and lives changed through the power of the Holy Spirit. Amen!

How do you describe RV Brown? A man with passion and love for God that is contagious. A man who loves his wife and is committed to raising his children God's way. I have personally known RV for several years and recognize his calling to reach youth and athletes with the gospel. He has a God-given ability to challenge, inspire, and encourage people of all ages to follow God. He has ministered in a variety of settings in our church and had a profound impact on many lives. RV is a big man with an even bigger heart. Plain and simple, he loves God with his whole heart, and he loves people. His faith is genuine, and his life continues to influence many to follow after Jesus Christ.

—Sr. Pastor Craig Altman
Grace Family Church
Lutz, Florida

Left: RV and Frances' children, Xavier and Sommer, all grown up.

"I have no greater joy than to hear that my children walk in truth."
(3 John 4)

Right: RV and his wife, Frances, are ONE in Christ.

"Husbands, likewise, dwell with them with understanding, giving honor to the wife, as to the weaker vessel, and as being heirs together of the grace of life, that your prayers may not be hindered."
(1 Peter 3:7)

Left: RV showing love to his nieces when they were little girls. Left to right: Paige, RV, and Courtney. The girls, now teenagers, live with their Uncle RV and Aunt Frances.

"Behold, children are a heritage from the LORD, the fruit of the womb is a reward."
(Psalm 127:3)

RV enjoys spending time with his family. Left to right: Courtney (niece), Xavier (son), Frances (wife), RV, Sommer (daughter), and Paige (niece).

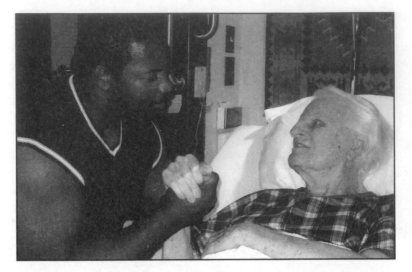

In June 2004, it was truly a prayer answered for RV to meet the world renowned evangelist, Dr. Billy Graham (in bed holding RV's hand) and fellowship with him. During this visit, RV had the opportunity to pray with and pray for Dr. Graham. This was one of the defining moments in RV's life. And, as the Apostle Paul did with Timothy in passing the torch to the next generation of believers, Dr. Graham, in response to RV's request, prayed for blessings upon RV's life, family, and ministry. Dr. Graham told RV to never compromise the calling God has placed on his life. Amen!

"But you be watchful in all things, endure afflictions, do the work of an evangelist, fulfill your ministry."

(2 Timothy 4:5)

Left to right: RV and Dr. Billy Graham. Now, the fire has been ignited!

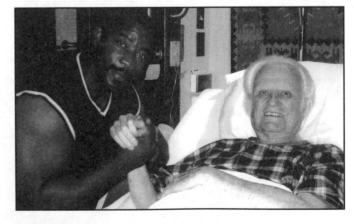

"Then I said, 'I will not make mention of Him, nor speak anymore in His name.' But His word was in my heart like a burning fire shut up in my bones; I was weary of holding it back, and I could not."

(Jeremiah 20:9)

Left to right: RV and Ann Graham Lotz share in the FCA's fiftieth anniversary celebration in February 2004. See the light that reflects off Ann and RV. Feel the presence of the Holy Ghost.

"For you were once darkness, but now you are light in the Lord. Walk as children of light (for the fruit of the Spirit is in all goodness, righteousness, and truth)."

(Ephesians 5:8–9)

Left to right: Dr. Danny Lotz and RV share a special moment at the home of Dr. Billy Graham.

"And they continued steadfastly in the apostles' doctrine and fellowship, in the breaking of bread, and in prayers."

(Acts 2:42)

RV stands with brothers who hold him accountable to love his family, and to read and share the Word of God. Left to right: Pastor Lurone Jennings Sr., Minister Gregory Beck, and RV. Every man needs accountability. These men have been with RV since 1982. They are mentors for other men as well.

"Therefore humble yourselves under the mighty hand of God, that He may exalt you in due time."

(1 Peter 5:6)

RV was inducted into the Fellowship of Christian Athletes Hall of Champions in October 2003. RV stands with brother and accountability partner, Sid Calloway, FCA Assistant State Director of Georgia.

ABOUT THE AUTHOR

E vangelist RV Brown is founder and President of Outreach to America's Youth, Inc. (O.T.A.Y.). RV received his Bachelor of Science degree from South Carolina State University. He played football all four years. He received certificates of training from Community Intervention, Inc., Minneapolis, Minnesota. He also received a certificate from Morehouse School of Medicine on drug abuse in the community.

RV taught special education for several years in the Chattanooga public school system. During that time he coached football and girls' basketball at Brainerd High School, he coached football, basketball, wrestling, and baseball at Howard High School, and he coached football at Hixson High School. He was voted Baseball Coach of the Year for Chattanooga City Schools in 1983.

RV accepted Jesus Christ as his Lord and Savior in November 1977. In 1988 the Lord called RV into full-time evangelism and gave him the vision to found Outreach to America's Youth, Inc. RV travels throughout the nation and abroad preaching the gospel of Jesus Christ. He carries the message of O.T.A.Y. to churches, prisons, retreats, camps, conferences, and college campuses. RV conducts *Breaking the Chain* school assemblies in middle and high schools. In 2003, RV received the honor of being inducted into the Fellowship of Christian Athletes (FCA) Hall of Champions.

RV Brown is the author of the *Breaking the Chain* workbook. This book is used to teach students in small-group settings.

Currently, RV resides in the Tampa, Florida area with his wife, Frances, their two children, Xavier and Sommer, and two nieces, Paige and Courtney.

To order additional copies of

STEP UP TO
THE PLATE,
DAD!

Have your credit card ready and call

Toll free: (877) 421-READ (7323)

or send $19.88* each, plus $5.95 S&H** to:

**RV Brown
P.O. Box 623
Odessa, FL 33556-0623**

Visit our website at www.rvbrown.com

*Florida residents, add 7% sales tax (tax = $1.39)

**add $1.50 S&H for each additional book ordered

100020

Overton Memorial Library
Step up to the plate, Dad! /
306.8742 B879s 2005

100020